The
CD-I PRODUCTION
Handbook

The CD-I Series

Introducing CD-I

This book provides a comprehensive non-technical overview of CD-I and is aimed at anyone interested in the implications of this revolutionary technology.

The CD-I Production Handbook

Aimed at the video and audio production teams involved in making CD-I titles, this book contains detailed examples exploring the concepts and central issues involved.

The CD-I Design Handbook

Aimed at designers with a technical background but no knowledge of CD-I, this book provides detailed, practical coverage of CD-I design. The different stages of CD-I design are richly illustrated with a wealth of examples.

The CD-I Programmer's Handbook

Aimed at CD-I programmers, this book is the standard programming manual on CD-I.

The official guide to CD-I Production
from Philips Interactive Media Systems

The CD-I PRODUCTION *Handbook*

PHILIPS IMS

ADDISON-WESLEY
PUBLISHING
COMPANY

Wokingham, England · Reading, Massachusetts · Menlo Park, California · New York
Don Mills, Ontario · Amsterdam · Bonn · Sydney · Singapore
Tokyo · Madrid · San Juan · Milan · Paris · Mexico City · Seoul · Taipei

© 1992 Philips Electronics UK Ltd

Many of the designations used by manufacturers and sellers to distinguish their products are claimed as trademarks. Addison-Wesley has made every attempt to supply trademark information about manufacturers and their products mentioned in this book. A list of the trademark designations and their owners appears on p. viii.

Cover designed by Chris Eley
and printed by The Riverside Printing Co. (Reading) Ltd.
Text designed by Valerie O'Donnell
Illustrations by Howie Twiner
Typeset by Electronic Type & Design, Oxford in 10/13 Candida and Futura
Printed in Great Britain by William Clowes, Beccles, Suffolk

First printed 1992.

ISBN 0–201–62750–7

Philips and Addison-Wesley would like to acknowledge TMS, Computer Authors for the initial draft, and Carol Atack for carrying out the final editing of this book. We would also like to thank the many reviewers who have contributed valuable comments as the project progressed and especially Clive Shepherd of EPIC Interactive and David Matthewson.

British Library Cataloguing in Publication Data
A catalogue record for this book is available from the British Library.

Library of Congress Cataloging in Publication Data

Preface

CD-I (Compact Disc Interactive, or interactive television) is a new medium and, as such, ways of working with it are still being developed. This book is aimed at anyone wishing to turn an idea for a CD-I disc into a programme that is ready to be played. It covers all the steps required to implement a CD-I design, with particular emphasis on practical opportunities and problems unique to CD-I.

Developing and producing a CD-I programme is a major project, which requires many skills. Some CD-I producers may be working on their own or as part of a small team whose members share most of the tasks and most of the skills required to complete them. Others will be part of a large enterprise in which each member of the team has a clearly defined and demarcated role; in this case the person who created the programme concept may have only a small role in the production process, and a team of designers and animators may create and finish parts of the programme from a design originated by a smaller team.

Modelling the design and production process

Most practitioners agree that CD-I is best served by beginning with a detailed design for a programme, testing the design as it is developed by prototyping and developing sample modules, and then proceeding to implement the design to produce the finished programme.

However, the design and production phases can never be fully separated. Apart from the fact that in many cases different stages will be worked on by the same people, each stage has to be informed by the requirements of others. It is, for example, no use creating a programme design that will prove to be impossible to produce. And those working on the production side need to be aware of the creative integrity of the design, and to involve designers if changes have to be made.

Although flexibility should be paramount throughout the design and production process, a structured way of working is vital because of the size of a CD-I project. Several hundred megabytes of data go on to the disc itself, while source materials can run to many times this, and are spread across many media. Good organization and a methodical way of working are vital during the production phase.

Who needs to know about CD-I production?

A wide range of staff can be involved in the production phase of CD-I. The designers and creative staff who came up with the original programme concept will probably still be involved in the project and will need to be aware of the constraints of the production process, both in creating the original design and amending it when required

Designers with specific skills, such as animators, will find that this book provides an overview of the entire process of which their work is a part. The same applies to picture editors, sound editors, programmers and other specialists.

Some CD-I programmes will feature newly recorded original material, whether sound or video, and the staff involved in producing this will need to know how their work is going to be used.

Finally, the producer or project manager, or whatever title is given to the managers who oversee the entire production process, should find that this book gives them an insight into their role and its demands.

Who should read this book?

This book is intended for all those working in the production of CD-I programmes, whatever their role, and also for those interested in commissioning CD-I material but unsure of what to expect. It should ideally be read in conjunction with the other books in the series, which provide further insights into particular aspects of CD-I. *Introducing CD-I* provides the type of information that potential producers, designers and those commissioning programmes are likely to want when first looking into CD-I. *The CD-I Design Handbook* is a source-book for designers, providing an introduction to designing interactive media, CD-I technology and its possibilities, and tips on working methods for CD-I designers. Finally, *The CD-I Programmer's Handbook* is a practical guide for CD-I programmers.

Contents

Contents

6 Gathering and converting materials 74

Contents

1

Producer and client

Introduction

Producing a CD-I is both a social and a technical process. It is a social process because making it involves cooperation between a large number of people from different backgrounds·with disparate skills, and because the product itself is intended to communicate information on behalf of a client to an intended audience. It is a technical process because it involves cooperation between a number of disciplines – from graphics to film-making and from software engineering to acting.

There is a further, practical split in CD-I production. First, in the general sense of the word production, there is the making of a CD-I programme from a carefully designed blueprint. However, in the film and television world on which the multi-media production world tends to model itself, production has a meaning both wider and more specific: it covers all stages of programme development, even those that do not directly result in the product. For the CD-I producer or manager the early stages of programme development, or preproduction, may be critical in producing a good result. Other staff may be more closely involved in the actual making of the programme, but still need to be aware of the ongoing process to which they are contributing.

The CD-I producer holds the threads of these skills and processes and ensures that all are woven into the finished product. There are many stages to be negotiated before a programme is completed, and although no project conforms to an exact blueprint there are many factors in common between them.

This chapter examines the earliest preproduction stages, and looks at the way CD-I discs are commissioned and the likely relationships between producer, client and designer. It also considers some of the resources needed for CD-I and ways in which the producer can find them.

Interactive television

A CD-I disc looks like an ordinary audio CD. The user simply slots the disc into the front of a CD-I player, and the programme starts. The designers of CD-I players have taken pains to make the interface between the audience and the player as simple as possible. It is fundamental to the concept of CD-I that it should never be hard to use.

The production values of CD-I should be as high as those to which the audience have grown accustomed in ordinary television. At the same time, CD-I offers several features that have not been available to a mass audience before. It is a type of **multimedia** and it is **interactive**.

'Multimedia' is a fashionable word. It means the possible combination of every type of music, speech, image, picture and text in one production. This doesn't sound unlike the sort of thing films do already. But the difference is that in multimedia all the media resources can be combined and recombined in a variety of ways. For example, in one CD-I the same picture of Nelson's column could be used for a travel feature about Trafalgar Square, a sympathetic look at the plight of pigeons, or a patriotic profile of Nelson.

Interactivity is also new to the mass market. Using a remote-control device very like the ones used to change channels on television, the audience can steer their way through the CD-I programme, making choices, deciding what they want to see, and in general tailoring the programme to meet their requirements exactly.

CD-I looks set to produce a small revolution in a variety of areas. Home entertainment and education need never be the same again. Now audiences are able to decide what they see and take a part in shaping their experience. In shops, schools, businesses and other locations, CD-I offers a quick and efficient way to present information and training materials. Students and customers can control the pace and content of the information aimed at them. The relatively low cost of the players and discs means that, with CD-I, the experience of interactive multimedia at last becomes accessible to everyone. People will be able to buy CD-I discs as they can records, videos and cassettes.

As the concept of CD-I becomes more widely known, demand for titles will increase. So also will the number of people and organizations who see CD-I as a suitable medium for their needs – either as a product in its own right, or as a way of carrying out some other task, such as publicity or training.

Between the people who wish to commission CD-I titles, for whatever purpose (clients), and the people who will use them, in whatever way (audience), are the people who bring CD-I titles into existence: designers and producers. The design process and the role of the designer is described in detail in the previous book in this series, *The CD-I Design Handbook*. This book describes the complementary and often overlapping roles and tasks of the CD-I producer.

The CD-I producer

The producer is the person responsible for realizing the CD-I design. The role of the CD-I producer is similar to that of the television producer. It may be that the person occupying the role goes under a different title, such as 'project manager', but this is a matter of taste or semantics, and not of substance. A producer coming from, say, a television background will have to become familiar with some of the disciplines of software production, while a project manager coming from a software background will have to learn some of the craft of the television producer. However, because of the nature of the medium the title 'producer' seems more appropriate than project manager. The task is to produce something and not merely to manage it.

Producing CD-I discs – not just the physical discs, but the programmes – is a new area of expertise. The CD-I producer has to be a jack of all trades – someone whose knowledge has to encompass a variety of areas, from sound-recording to software engineering, and from animation to video techniques, with project management and public-relations skills thrown in for good measure. This means that producing a CD-I title or series of titles can be a complex task.

For the purposes of this book, we have identified two aspects of each process involved: the process itself (for example: obtaining sound recordings in a suitable format) and the management of the process (for example: using project-management techniques to ensure that deadlines are properly scheduled and met). The book divides into two sections, one on each aspect. It will help the producer to identify and coordinate all the strands involved in the production process, so that he or she follows a smooth and trouble-free path to a product in the shops, a satisfied client and an interested audience.

Client relations

One of the first tasks that is likely to exercise the CD-I producer is liaison with the client, or between the client and the designers. Negotiating the contract, agreeing the budget and working out who will provide what equipment and material will be an important task for CD-I producers.

CD-I does not exist in a commercial vacuum. Every CD-I project, as with most other enterprises, exists because someone has seen a need for it in the market and plans to fulfil that need, either directly or by engaging a specialist producer to do so. With what sorts of people or organizations might a CD-I producer become involved?

There are few limitations on who can hope to make a CD-I. At the less ambitious end of the spectrum, a Philips starter system enables even the smallest organizations or individuals to produce quite impressive multimedia presentations for a very modest outlay. At the ambitious end, professional studios, equipped with networked workstations, proper audio and video facilities and a team of people with the relevant skills, can produce blockbuster titles, but using the sorts of budget associated with film or television production.

Here are a few examples of the sort of people or organizations that might wish to produce CD-I titles:

- a sales training company, to add interest and realism to its training courses – and to promote itself to potential customers;
- a publishing house specializing in partworks, to issue a series of CD-I titles on dress-making, which will appear monthly;
- a company whose exciting new product needs demonstration and explanation, by means of highly visual point-of-sale information in High Street stores;
- an entertainment conglomerate with a large catalogue of material, seizing the chance to exploit the initial interest in a new medium and to gain a strong position in the market as it grows.

The producer can be involved with clients in any of these situations. From the producer's point of view there is always a client, whether it's a third party or the product manager within the CD-I team's own company. Even if the production activity is being carried out in-house there will be a person who can say things like 'no more money' or 'no more time' or 'it doesn't look right' or, more optimistically, 'great' .

It's important to remember that the client and the audience for the programme are not necessarily one and the same, although the client should usually know who the audience will be – for example, new staff, shoppers or geography students. In some cases, however, the CD-I producer may be selling a programme concept and its potential audience as a package to an investor. It may be more critical for design staff to be aware of the audience's needs and for the production staff to be aware of the client's needs, but of course, neither side of the team can afford to be ignorant of either set of requirements.

The importance of the client
It is worth remembering that from the producer's point of view there is always a client. Even if the production activity is being carried out in-house there should be someone who takes the role of the client.

Finding and allocating resources

An important task for the CD-I producer is finding and allocating the resources for production. There are several types of resources, and each may be provided by either client or producer, although the client will end up paying for them.

Whoever they are, and whatever the size of their organization, producers working for clients who are getting involved with CD-I production need to consider several factors:

- What resources does the client already have?
- What resources does the producer already have?
- What resources will need to be provided for this project?

By 'resources' are meant such things as:

- People. The CD-I producer is likely to be selling the skills of design and production staff to clients. But some clients may already have staff who will work on the CD-I. For example, a television company will probably have audiovisual production and editing staff who can work on the production of the CD-I programme, preparing new material for inclusion.

- Materials. Clients may possess suitable materials, such as publicity photographs or slide libraries, to use in the programme, or new material may need to be sourced.

- Equipment. The client may already have studio facilities for recording and editing material, or a department equipped to produce graphics. It's unlikely that there will be a full CD-I studio already in place at the client's premises, and most CD-I producers will be charging clients for use of their facilities, or for third-party facilities houses and specialist CD-I studios used for the project.

Knowing who is contracted to provide what resources is essential before production can begin, so that the production process can be adequately planned and it is clear who is responsible for what, and when it must be ready.

The production process

Once client and producer are agreed, work may begin, or continue with fresh enthusiasm and more cash. The design will be fleshed out from the original concept or treatment, and the contribution specialist staff can make will become clearer.

There is no one right way of going about CD-I production. It is still a relatively new art and there are almost as many approaches to the subject as there are practitioners. People have arrived in CD-I with all sorts of backgrounds, from CBT (Computer-Based Training) to television production, from software engineering to animation. This is bound to affect their conception of the process. Possibly a television producer will run the project in a more obviously creative way than a software engineer. The results may appear very similar in the end, but the routes that led up to them may have been quite different.

However, it is possible to pick out some essential features of any approach, and that is what this book tries to do.

Events and tasks

The sequence of events that results in a CD-I looks something like this:

- concept
- outline
- detailed design
- creation of materials
- authoring
- disc-building
- testing
- replication

The *concept* is the idea for the product. It could come from a company or from an individual, who could be a fully fledged interactive-media designer.

The *outline* is a more detailed treatment of the idea. This would have to be worked on by someone with a thorough understanding of the technicalities of CD-I.

The *detailed design* is the specification for the product. At this stage, if the project is a fairly ambitious one, all the specialist skills of scriptwriters, subject specialists and software engineers will be called upon.

Creation of materials – sometimes known as assets – then proceeds. This may simply be running odd bits of artwork through a flatbed scanner, or it may involve extensive location filming and recording in sound studios, as well as the creation of specialist chunks of software to power the programme.

Authoring is the drawing together of pictures and sounds and imposing the desired programme structure on them.

Disc-building is the process of putting all the materials together on the disc in the most aesthetically satisfying and efficient way.

Testing, which goes on throughout the whole process, comes to its climax when the materials have been assembled into a version of the final disc and are run. There should be no surprises at this stage, but this is when the product is seen as a whole for the first time.

Replication is the process of manufacturing as many copies of the disc as are required. An essential feature of this stage is the production of packaging and label art.

For the producer, CD-I production is the process of bringing the title described in the detailed design specification into being. The detailed design specification is the end result of the design process (described in the previous book in this series). It is a complete blueprint from which the CD-I can be made. It includes a script and a software specification, as well as timescales and budgets. Once everything has been specified on paper in this way, the production process proper is ready to begin.

Here are the elements that are common to the production phase of most CD-I projects:

- production of software
- producing, and managing the production of, the control program
- production of materials
- producing, and managing the production of, video, audio, graphic and other materials
- legal matters
- researching and negotiating any rights, copyrights and so on
- physical production processes
- organizing and scheduling the production of the CD-I discs, their cases, packaging and labels
- staff management
- team or project management

The tasks are not sequential, but run parallel and overlap each other. For example, you might have to start thinking about packaging and distribution quite early on in the production process, well before you have a product to package and distribute, whereas team management lasts throughout the project.

Production staff who are not directly involved in the design stage may be working on a range of preproduction tasks, such as booking production facilities, finding any extra staff needed to work on the project, and acquiring rights for any existing material that may be used in the programme.

Tools for CD-I production

As we saw earlier with the examples of different types of clients and production arrangements, the process of making CD-I titles can take place on quite a few levels. The complexity of the title is matched by the complexity or simplicity of the tools involved in putting the production together, or authoring it.

Although there is really a continuum between the most ambitious projects, employing batteries of C-programmers, and lightweight productions involving the use of a relatively inexpensive one-piece authoring kit, for the purposes of this manual it may be convenient to distinguish two sorts of production environment:

- environment 1: simple authoring tools, such as a Philips starter system; for straightforward slide and music presentations.

- environment 2: anything from slightly more complex authoring tools – PC- and Mac-based authoring systems – to powerful workstations and libraries of tools and utilities (such as Philips' Balboa); for productions involving more complex effects such as animation and full-motion video (see Chapter 5), and ambitious projects involving the development or utilization of software engines.

In spite of the fact that in many cases tools from either environment may be used (for example, prototyping for quite a sophisticated production might be done on a Philips starter system), this is a useful distinction to make. In Chapter 5, when CD-I effects are described, this distinction will be used to indicate the environment in which the effects are created and controlled.

Some idea of which sort of environment your project is likely to use will help you to decide what effects are possible and how they will be achieved. This is, of course, a factor that should have been taken into account at the design stage. But it is also useful for the producer and production team to have some idea of what they can offer to do or wisely avoid.

Conclusion

The successful production of a CD-I programme requires more than a good programme concept. It is a large project requiring many disparate resources, which need to be carefully organized to make sure that the programme is finished to the satisfaction of both its designers and the clients who commissioned it.

There are many different tasks within the production process, some of which will be carried out by specialists and some of which will be the responsibility of the overall producer or manager. A good producer will be beginning work as the design is being created, organizing resources for the production stages to come, ensuring that both production and design staff and the client are fully aware of who is committed to what tasks, and establishing beneficial liaison between the client and the design and production staff.

Working out the budget for the programme, marshalling and allocating resources, including staff, equipment and facilities, and ensuring that legal matters such as the contract to make the programme and the rights to use pre-existing material are all in place, are the essential parts of the preproduction stage.

2

Setting up a CD-I studio

Introduction

Starting out in CD-I production will often require at least some investment in software and systems, as well as the staff to run them. If existing staff are going to learn how to create and produce CD-I programmes they will need training. New staff will need to be assessed for their potential with the new medium.

Acquiring equipment when you are not yet entirely sure of your needs is always difficult and CD-I is no exception. This chapter looks at some of the problems that face the producer or manager setting up the facilities for a first CD-I development project.

Equipping your studio

It's impossible to do any job without the appropriate tools, but there are surprisingly few specialist tools required in CD-I. In many cases, computer hardware and software needed to develop and produce the programme will already be in use for other graphics projects. Little of the equipment need be specific to CD-I work, although there is a wide range of dedicated hardware and software available if required.

Figure 2.1 The Philips CD-I Emulator, contained in the central cabinet here, is a comprehensive disc-building and programme emulation system, which can run on most Sun, Macintosh or PC-compatible computers. It is part of a workstation that includes a computer (left) and a CD-I system (right).

Hardware

Most dedicated CD-I tools are available for use on a variety of hardware platforms, including Sun workstations, Apple Macintosh and IBM-compatible personal computers. This can substantially reduce the start-up costs of getting involved in CD-I production. If your studio already contains suitable computers, you won't need to buy any more.

Storage

What CD-I does require is massive storage, and you may find that you do need to invest in extra hard drives and back-up space. A full CD-I disc can hold 650 megabytes of data, and during production there may be many times this amount requiring storage, even if only temporarily. Remember that much of the material that goes onto the disc is compressed to save space, and that at some point in its life it won't be compressed. Newly created animations and newly digitized photographs are just

some of the aspects of CD-I that can use disc space. The final
stages of building and testing the disc image will also need lots
of accessible disc space – one programming manager reckons
that four or five times the size of the finished programme is
about right.

Emulation

There are pieces of dedicated CD-I equipment that you will
need. A CD-I emulator allows a programme under development
to be played as if it were a finished and pressed CD-I disc. It's a
vital part of CD-I development and, unless your involvement in
CD-I is likely to be short-term, is something that the production
and validation team will require regular access to. The use of the
emulator is described in more detail in Chapter 10.

Dedicated development systems

Some producers may come to CD-I with little previous experience of computer systems, and it may be more appropriate for
them to acquire one of the several dedicated CD-I development
systems. Some of these, such as Philips' starter systems, are
aimed at new CD-I producers who want to get a feel for the
medium without investing too much in computer equipment.

Software

As with hardware, many non-dedicated multimedia and graphics
application packages can easily be used for CD-I production.
Deciding whether to use existing software or special CD-I
software, where the choice exists, is a matter entirely of individual preference. Many graphics packages can produce output acceptable to CD-I – for example, Adobe's PhotoShop
application for the Apple Macintosh.

If the designers are used to a tool and it can work with CD-I
it may be pointless to move to a new and different package. On
the other hand, it's worth keeping an open mind and looking at
as much of the available software as possible; a new program,

or a new version of an existing one, may offer a new capability or function that could be just what your project needs.

Standard programs may be useful for other aspects of CD-I development and production. Spreadsheets and project management software may keep a project in budget and on time. Databases may be useful for storing information of many kinds, logging assets and maintaining programme records. Hypermedia tools may be useful to programme designers for quick explorations of programme structure and simple prototypes.

Authoring tools

Much of this book is about the use of CD-I authoring tools. Authoring is the process that turns all the material and assets that have been gathered into the CD-I programme that you have designed. It is a major component of CD-I production and selecting the right authoring environment for the projects you will be working on is very important.

Experienced CD-I producers believe that it's important to have 'room to grow' in any authoring software that you use. Too simple a package may offer too few facilities for the programmes you want to make next. However, authoring packages are increasingly sophisticated and each revision imposes fewer limitations on the user.

What is important about any software is that people should really know how to use it. Working with unfamiliar software will add a substantial burden to the project workload and reduce the efficiency of staff. Before investing in any major production or design tools, check that training and support are available (and remember to budget for them).

Chapter 7 contains much more detail about choosing and using authoring software.

Networking

Joining computers together as part of a network can add greatly to the efficiency of the studio. It enables work in progress to be stored and managed centrally, and transferred between staff

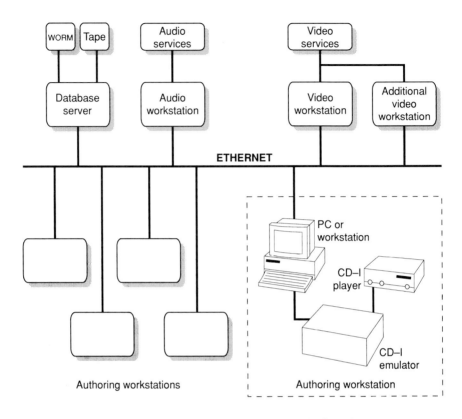

Figure 2.2 Typical layout of a networked studio.

more easily, as well as offering the traditional advantages of easier access to peripherals such as printers. Figure 2.2 shows a simplified diagram of how a production studio could be organized as a network.

Alternative facilities

It's not always necessary to buy in all the equipment that will be used. The television industry has come to rely upon independently owned production facilities that give producers access to equipment that it wouldn't be cost-effective to own outright. CD-I can operate in the same way; studio facilities are being established and can be hired in the same way as linear television facilities. The latter may also prove useful to CD-I production teams who don't have access to in-house studios and editing suites.

For example, audio-visual segments of a programme may need to be recorded even though they form only a small part of the planned programme. For most CD-I producers it will almost certainly be cheaper to hire a studio, the equipment and any extra specialist staff needed for this part of programme production. Editing audio-visual material prior to digitizing it for use in the CD-I programme may also be done in more conventional studios.

Dedicated CD-I studios can also be hired, with or without the use of specialist staff to assist in production. Using such facilities may prove particularly valuable for newcomers to CD-I as it can provide a valuable introduction both to good CD-I working practices and to a range of CD-I equipment. Occasional CD-I producers may find it simpler to hire such facilities as necessary rather than to invest in software and equipment that will rarely be used.

Human resources

The staff who will design and develop CD-I programmes are among the most vital assets a production house can have. A good team in which everyone works well together will contribute a large amount to the success of a studio and its projects.

The differing mix of skills needed as projects progress from start to finish may mean that in practice only a core team works in the studio full-time, being supplemented by specialist contractors or temporary staff as each project requires. There's no point in paying an expensive programmer if none of the projects

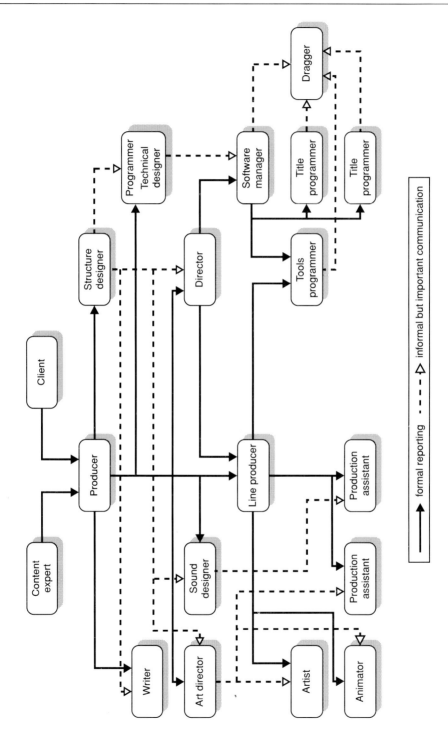

Figure 2.3 Job titles in CD-I production.

over the next year requires anything other than feeding material through a set of ready-gathered programme templates. Figure 2.3 shows the kinds of roles likely to be involved in a project as it journeys from concept to completion, and the relationships between the roles.

Each project will require different mixes of skills, and all but the simplest of CD-I programmes will need at least one of the following. A typical arrangement is for a representative of each type of skill to be involved from the very beginning of a project, and for these people to build up small teams and manage them during the more demanding production phase.

Graphics and design staff

Graphics are a major part of any CD-I programme. Whether they consist of still images, animations, or attractive graphics on a menu screen, the overall look of a programme is vital to its success.

Designers working in CD-I need to be aware of the restrictions and the possibilities the medium creates. Previous experience in television graphics will be useful, but it's probably more important that designers can get to grips with and respond to the CD-I technology, and interpret material for this new medium.

Content specialists

As with traditional television programmes, someone needs to take responsibility for the detail of the programme content, to research the subject to make sure that the best material is included, and to ensure that nothing has been left out or any good opportunities for the programme missed.

While the programme producer should take overall responsibility for this, the finer details are better delegated to experienced researchers who can also deal with important questions such as acquiring rights for the use of material not owned by the production company or client.

Interactive designers

Interactivity is what makes CD-I and other forms of interactive television different from more traditional media. Designing programmes that take full advantage of this additional dimension is an invaluable skill that must be represented on the CD-I team.

There have been various forms of interactive multimedia in use over the years, and there are a few people who have learned a great deal about interactive design. For some CD-I producers, however, there may be no-one on the team who combines a grasp of both the technical and the creative sides of CD-I. In this case teamwork becomes more important and can enable all these different bases to be covered.

Recruiting and managing programmers

Most media have always needed technical staff, to help maintain equipment and train their colleagues in its use. As a new medium, CD-I is more reliant on individual technical expertise, not just to keep the machines working but to make the programme work as well.

If you need to recruit a programmer or to brief someone else to recruit them, what should you look for? An experienced CD-I software development manager put it like this:

> 'I find the kind of people we want are very unusual; the key thing is that people should have real-time experience. The perception is that you want people who have graphics experience, but the problems we're facing all the time are real-time problems. So good experience of real-time programming, preferably on 68000 or even OS-9, is more important than graphics experience, or even knowledge of C for that matter, provided someone has a good knowledge of programming languages.'

Another CD-I programming manager believes that while experience of real-time work is important, the ideal CD-I programmer will also understand issues in graphics and user interface design, and be interested in entertainment, film and music. 'We often find that good CD-I programmers come from a computer games background,' he says.

Most importantly, programmers should be able to communicate well with non-technical staff, and share their aspirations for the programme. This is particularly important, because good CD-I design practice suggests that programmers are involved at all stages of the design and production process, and if members of each discipline can understand the requirements of the other specialisms involved in CD-I development, it will be a great help in getting the work done.

Line and overall management

Clear leadership and direction are important for any project. But with so many disciplines participating in CD-I, what should the background of the project leader or manager be? And should the creative management be in the same hands as the project management and administration?

The answers will vary from project to project. The amount of business administration to be dealt with will vary from company to company; a small independent CD-I producer will probably have more to deal with than one who is part of a large, established media production company with separate departments to handle such matters. In some companies, a split in responsibilities between a producer, responsible for management issues, and a director, responsible for the creative side of the project, may be appropriate. In others the producer may take a much more active role in the creation and development of the programme.

One CD-I designer affirms that the best person to lead the team is the interactive designer, who has the most experience of the medium and the problems that are likely to arise, as well as being in a better position to develop realistic schedules for programme development and production.

Conclusion

Producing a CD-I requires staff and facilities, and in most cases these will need to be in place before the project begins. Both the people who will work on a programme and the equipment they will use need to be booked and organized, and making all the necessary arrangements in good time will in most cases fall to the producer or the project management team.

With so many resources needed for a programme, skilful management and shepherding of resources are needed to keep facility hire to a minimum and expensive contract staff fully occupied while they are working on a project. Acquiring the right resources is only half of the picture; the next chapter discusses the management of the project and its resources in more detail.

3
Managing a CD-I project

Introduction

Project management is a vital skill for CD-I production. Because of its complexity, a typical CD-I development project requires considerable effort to be put into scheduling and organization. While these organizational skills will be familiar to anyone who has managed any kind of development project, the sheer diversity of effort created by multimedia means that there is a lot of information for the manager to keep on top of. Orchestrating each individual contribution to the project to ensure that the whole is finished on time and within budget can become very difficult. The producer will need both management skills and an understanding of CD-I development to make sure that both promises and demands made are achievable and that staff have not been committed to producing the impossible.

Good project management is also important for the financial side of the production process. Payment for large projects is generally made in stages and linked to satisfactory completion of each project stage. Project milestones need to be identified, scheduled and then met.

Milestones

It is important that both producer and client are clear as to what work constitutes each stage and what the outcome of each stage is supposed to be.

For this reason, it is usual to agree project milestones in advance. A milestone is a major point in the project and is usually defined precisely. So, for instance, 'when the design work is finished' is rather too vague an expression to be a milestone written into the contract. There is scope for disagreement over whether the design work is indeed finished, and when this happened. Instead, the milestone should be something more concrete, such as 'delivery of the detailed design specification document'. This not only clarifies precisely which part of the design work must be completed, but also ties the agreement down to a specific document. It's probably more useful to focus on *delivery* of a document or product as the milestone rather than *acceptance* of the same if money is involved.

The specific outcomes of each stage of a project are referred to as 'deliverables'. The word is rather unwieldy but clearly expresses a concept that is useful for large, complex projects. Specifying them helps to focus the production team on what they must actually produce, and gives the clients a clear idea of what they can expect and when.

A discussion of what the deliverables will be, entered into at the project planning stage, can also bring to light any mutual misunderstanding that exists between different parties to the contract. The more clearly the deliverables are defined the less likely there is to be confusion when it comes to delivery and payment.

As a CD-I project moves through its different stages, it will have various milestones and deliverables. An example of such a series of milestones is shown in Table 3.1. This is an example, not a formula. The stages, the milestones and the deliverables will vary greatly from one project to another. The important thing is to agree them in advance, so that both sides are clear as to what they are. It's also important to agree realistic dates at which milestones are to be reached, and this will form a large part of the scheduling process. Figure 3.1 shows the stages a project can go through and the personnel involved in each stage.

Table 3.1 An example of a project milestones document.

Stage	Milestone	Deliverable
Concept and treatment	Approval of outline treatment and initial budget	Outline treatment document
Detailed design	Review/approval of design document	Detailed design document HyperCard prototype
	Project plan	Plan and budget documents
	Detailed budgets	
A-V material origination	Review/approval of all A-V materials in non-CD-I format Final budget	Video on Betacam SP $\frac{1}{4}$" audiotapes Final budget document
Authoring/ programming	Review/approval of emulator version	WORM from emulator corrections
Production	Review/approval of title on WORM disc	WORM disc for testing and review
Final stage	Delivery of master title to CD-I plant	Disc image on Exabyte tape or WORM

Scheduling

Breaking down a project into milestones is one part of scheduling. It's difficult to avoid a chicken-and-egg situation in which the production schedule can't be worked out until the milestones have been established and the milestones can't be agreed upon because there's no schedule to work out dates by which they should be reached. Experience will solve this problem by providing rules of thumb for how long any given stage of a project is likely to take.

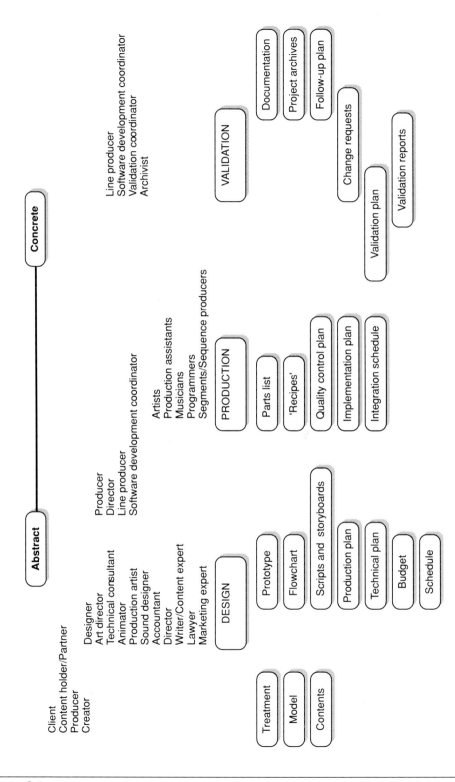

Figure 3.1 Jobs and people involved at various stages of production.

If you are new to CD-I production, scheduling may seem a daunting task. But it need not be. The critical task is to break the project into clear stages, and to get the staff most involved in that stage to estimate the work and the time that will be necessary.

Don't be afraid to use other people's expertise. For instance, if you are intending to have the work produced in a CD-I studio, the production staff will be used to giving detailed estimates of how long various processes will take. Be prepared for the studio to ask lots of detailed questions about the precise format of your CD-I design. The more information you can give them, the more accurately they will be able to estimate the time the job will take.

You may end up with a large chunk of time on the schedule that is simply labelled 'authoring'. The software development manager can usually take over from here, supplying you with details of how the work is going to be broken down. Some software managers use a technique of first breaking down the work to be done into a number of work packages.

One large project consisted of 40–50 work packages, spread over about six months. In general, one person worked on one work package at a time, but sometimes a very experienced programmer had a secondary role, acting as back-up to one who was less experienced.

In this kind of project each work package tends to be associated with a software module or 'manager'. In the case of very complex software modules, the work packages are in fact sub-modules.

A software development manager describes how this process is managed in terms of time:

> 'You always need to allow plenty of time for slippages. You frequently come across a production technique that is being used for the first time, like using a new conversion routine, or you may be taking assets from a source that you've never used before. So I always plan that people start working with placeholder data and then integrate with real data and I'll try not to make that point too critical in the plan. That's perhaps not an unusual concept for people who've worked in video.'

It is often difficult to find a rule of thumb for use in estimating. Another software development manager does it this way:

'There's always a requirement for a substantial amount of time in integration and testing. Because it's a real-time system, that application is very constrained by memory or bandwidth and optimization always takes a lot of time. The idea of a three-thirds breakdown seems about right:

- one-third specification
- one-third coding
- one-third integration and testing

So for a large project I might plan for perhaps three people to work on it at the start, and then at the end perhaps taper it off so as to leave one person doing the testing and optimization. In practice, that's quite often the nasty bit and several people for a short period of time isn't the most effective way to handle it, because it requires someone who understands it in depth. This is especially true for consumer titles, which really have to be slick.'

The 'don't be afraid to ask' rule also applies with CD-I pressing. The plant will be able to give you a very precise idea of how long the job will take. The other parts of the project lie in more familiar territory. Many artists and designers will be prepared to quote a fixed number of days for a job. However, beware the complication of elapsed time, discussed next.

Elapsed time

Suppose an artist quotes 10 days' work to produce some graphics screens. It seems reasonable and you accept the quotation, building the 10 days into the schedule for the project. What the artist has forgotten to tell you is that after the first five days' work, colour transparencies will need to be sent off for special processing, so the job will be on hold until they come back.

In fact, although this job will take 10 days of the artist's time it will occupy three weeks of elapsed time because of the wait in the middle. The days that someone quotes for a job are far more an indication of how much the job will cost than they are of how long it will take. Factors that affect the elapsed time for a project can include:

- Waiting periods: for example, a particular programmer or artist may have to wait for a piece of equipment to become available, for a piece of outside processing to be finished or for a review/approval of one part of the work to be completed.
- Problems: these might involve redesigning something because the design doesn't work in practice, having to redo work that does not meet quality assurance standards or equipment breaking down or proving unable to cope with the level of work it has to do.
- Personal factors: anything that can affect people's productivity, such as illness, holidays, changes of job, learning time and so on.
- The calendar: weekends and holiday periods.
- Contingencies: the office ceiling falls down and so on.

Because it is important for materials to arrive at the CD-I studio on a set date, the calculation of the elapsed time is a vital part of the project planning. In practice, lots of the processes will run simultaneously.

It may help the initial 'back of an envelope' project plan to compile one or more summary sheets for each stage of the project (Table 3.2). These can list the planning information about that stage of the project.

Table 3.2 Project plan schedule.

Stage	Prepare graphics for delivery to studio
Time (workdays)	10
Cost	£2000.00
Elapsed time	3 weeks
Start date	7th June
End date	28th June

Next you can plot these against a calendar, to get an idea of which activities will run together, which are dependent on each other and so on. Figure 3.2 shows the kind of diagram you might produce. Whether you use a high-tech computer or a low-tech pencil and eraser, be prepared to keep changing the schedule until it is correct.

| 22 Nov 90 | GANTT CHART | Page 1 |
| | PROJECT TITLE | |

November 1990 ---+--- December 1990 ---+--- January 1991 ---+--- February 1991---+---

|Day|Resrc| 29 | 5 | 12 | 19 | 26 | 3 | 10 | 17 | 24 | 31 | 7 | 14 | 21 | 28 | 4 | 11 | 18 | 25 |

Activity	Day	Resrc
Technical specification	19	BN
Menu scroll routine	16	KC
Picture tools	8	KC
Test disc	3	KC
Hotspot definition and highlighting	3	BN
Vertical menus	8	BN
Segmented buffer manager	5	BN
Cut-out sprites	2	SP
Soft cursor manager	10	SP
Menu fast forward	10	KC
A-V manager	43	JW AT
A-V RTF build	2	JW
Real-time record manager	3	JW
Miscellaneous section	5	JW
Integration and test	15	JW BN

Legend

-----	Activity	L----	Locked activity
C----	Activity on critical path	^	Original planned start date
-----	Partially completed activity	v	Original planned end date
▄▄▄▄	Completed activity	.....	Discontinuous activity

Figure 3.2 Typical schedule for a project. After each process or item that must be produced, the time required is listed, and then the initials of the responsible person. Activities lying on the critical path are crucial because delays in them will delay the following activities.

Budgeting

There are broadly two ways of budgeting. One way is to propose a design, find out how long everything is going to take and how much it will cost, and finally present this figure to the client. The other is for the client to say 'What can you do for £25,000?' and for you to work backwards, to a design that will be feasible within that budget.

In practice, most project budgets evolve from a mixture of these two methods. Discussions begin on a very general level, then gradually become more specific as the expectations of each side become clearer.

Linking the budget to the milestones in the schedule enables the cash flow to be drawn up. This shows both you and the client when money will be needed and helps both parties to plan any staged payments for the project. It is usual as part of the contract to specify exact payments, linked to milestones and deliverables. Table 3.3 is an example from a real project.

Table 3.3 Payment schedule.

30%	of estimated initial budget upon placing the order
20%	of final project budget on completion of the detailed design stage
25%	at conclusion of month 3 from delivery of detailed design
balance	1 month from delivery of the final master disc for validation

Clearly, it is difficult to provide detailed budgetary information when you haven't yet gone into the design issues in enough detail. Examining them in this kind of depth is probably part of the brief for the detailed design stage. So it is common for costs to be estimated in the project proposal. Following agreement on the proposal and on the appropriate payments according to the payment schedule, work on the detailed design stage begins. The team uses the information that becomes available as the detailed design stage progresses, in order to draw up final project budgets and plans. Again, the team may moderate the design in the light of the budget they know they're working with.

Once again, the budget will go to the client for approval, before the final stage starts. As with the time budgets, it is important to be realistic and to make allowances for problems.

The extract that follows is from an actual proposal. This section is detailing the way that comments on the review of the WORM version of the CD-I will be dealt with after the testing phase:

> 'The costs of any program modifications outside the bounds of the original detailed design will be estimated during this phase and appropriate modification proposals submitted as required.
>
> Software "fixes" within the guidelines outlined in the detailed design specification will, of course, be included in the final project budget submitted at the conclusion of the detailed design phase.'

This CD-I producer is making sure that the final project budget, prepared and submitted after the detailed design stage, makes quite clear which amendments or 'fixes' could be carried out within the budget. However, if the client is prepared to bear the extra cost, then additions and changes that were not originally specified can, of course, be carried out.

It is important to get this kind of thing straight because it is the type of issue that can lead to misunderstanding and disagreement. To make things crystal-clear, the producer added an 'either/or' milestone for this stage:

> 'Milestone: *either* agreement that the WORM performs according to the specification presented in the detailed design
>   *or*
> a detailed design and budget for specific program changes required.'

In most contracts there is also provision for the event of a rejected deliverable. This usually stipulates that reasons for the rejection must be given by the client and a plan for resubmission prepared by the producer.

Rights and copyright clearances

Those institutions and companies that have clear title and copyright to materials that would make attractive CD-Is are clearly in a very strong position as the market expands. As the industry develops, 'Who owns the rights?' will become a key question for producers and it is one they must address early on in the production process if they are to avoid problems.

It is likely with some titles that one of the production team will spend the whole life of the project researching rights and getting legal clearances, as well as finding materials in archives and libraries. The nature of this research is the same as in conventional video but the scale of the task is quite different because of the far larger volumes of data that can be held on CD-I.

This has budget implications, and it is always worth finding out whether commissioning original audio-visual material may not be a cheaper option. For other titles the client may be supplying much of the material. If this is the case the client should be able to guarantee ownership of the material; it is, however, worth checking that even publicity material is properly available for use in CD-I. Copyright clearance should be signed off at a very high level because the consequences of infringing copyright can be serious.

The team should be thinking about copyright issues at the very start of the design process. It would be foolish, for example, to sell a client a training programme centred on the idea of the training being led by a famous cartoon character if it were unlikely that the cartoon's creators would be willing to license the character for use in such a programme.

Conclusion

Good management makes the task of CD-I production much easier. A thoroughly prepared and realistic schedule is needed to keep the project on track, to let all the team assess progress and put in extra effort where necessary, and to give the clients a clearer indication of the work being done on their behalf.

Scheduled project milestones, simply to mark progress or to trigger staged payments, provide a direction for a project and allow the team's energies to be usefully focused on an achievable short- or medium-term goal. The more clearly milestones and the deliverables that they comprise are defined, the more useful they are.

Equally, it's important that the development and production team retain a vision of the project as a whole. The shape and tone of the programme must not be lost because it has become too compartmentalized, so that staff working on each section are not able to see where their work fits into the project as a whole.

4

CD-I: the medium, the player and the disc

Introduction

Looking at some of the technical features of CD-I helps in understanding the production process. If you are already familiar with how CD-I works, and the effects available, you should skip this chapter or just use it to jog your memory. For full information on the technical aspects of CD-I you should consult *CD-I Full Functional Specification*, also known as the Green Book, the authoritative reference to CD-I hardware supplied with CD-I development systems.

For the producer, there is more to know than that the CD-I disc slots into the CD-I player and plays a title. Bear in mind that both the disc and the player are finite resources. That is to say, the disc can hold only a fixed amount of material, and the player can take only a fixed, limited amount of material off the disc at a time. The disc is like a bucket holding the multimedia materials required by the title, and the player is like a funnel through which the material pours (Figure 4.1).

The detailed physical design specification will already have taken care of such issues as how much material will be stored on the disc, and how fast the player will need to read it. However, the production process will be to some extent an interactive and iterative one, with producers and designers consulting together on how to achieve the design within the resources available. This will particularly be the case in the small percentage of applications that use all the space on the

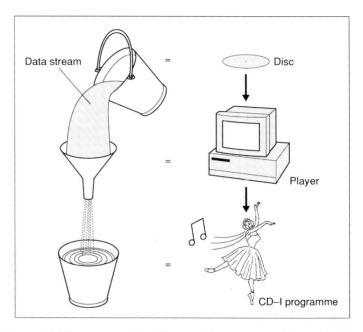

Figure 4.1 The rate at which data can be transferred from the disc to the player is limited.

disc. If disc space is this tight, the producer may have to adjudicate between rival claims for space or make decisions that will optimize the use of the available space. Knowing the technical possibilities and alternatives is important in making these kinds of choices.

The medium

CD-I is a digital medium. Everything on the disc – pictures, music, text – is represented by numbers. For example, the brightness and colour of every part of a picture are translated into bytes of computer code. The numbers are stored as pits and bumps on the surface of the disc and are read by a laser beam. This is important because it means that all materials that are put onto the disc either have to be recorded in a digital form suitable for CD-I discs to start with, or have to be converted into digital form later on.

Digital media are commonly contrasted with analogue media. An analogue medium is one in which a picture or a sound is recorded directly and not coded into numbers. For example, when rays of light pass through the lens of a camera and reproduce a scene by affecting chemicals on the surface of the film, that is an analogue process. Analogue processes are smooth and continuous, while digital processes are discrete and discontinuous.

Digital media have several advantages over analogue media:

- They can be accurately reproduced without loss of quality. This means that large numbers of copies can be made without any reduction in quality.
- Mathematical techniques can compress the amount of data (numerical information) used to record a sound or a picture. This means you can get more material on a disc.
- Electronic editing techniques can be used to produce effects that are far more difficult to obtain by other means. This means that sounds, pictures, and so on, can be adjusted until they exactly serve the required purpose, in a way that is far more awkward when analogue techniques are used.
- Different media can be stored in a common form in the same place (a picture and the sound that goes with it can sit right next to each other in neighbouring sectors of a CD-I disc).

The anatomy of the player

The CD-I player box looks like a very straightforward piece of consumer electronics. But in fact, inside (like many domestic electrical goods these days) it is very sophisticated. It contains decoders to read material from the disc, find out what type of information it is and then convert it into sound, image or text as required. This information is then either played or displayed

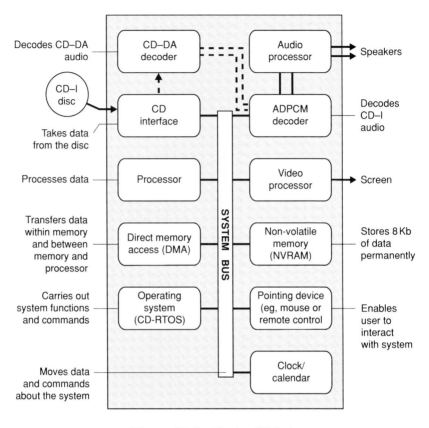

Figure 4.2 Inside the CD-I player.

immediately, or held in the player's memory until it is requested by the programme or the viewer. Software built into the system ensures that all these processes take place in the correct order. Figure 4.2 shows the functional parts of the CD-I player.

Parts of the player

CD-DA decoder

Decodes signals from ordinary CD audio discs, and CD-quality sound stored on CD-I discs. Sound signals are played as they come off the disc.

ADPCM decoder

The Adaptive Delta Pulse Code Modulator decodes audio signals from specifically CD-I discs. Again, sound signals are played as they come off the disc.

Video decoder

Decodes video signals for most visual material except full-motion video. Video signals are held in the system's one megabyte of random-access memory, and synchronized with the sounds by the software on the disc.

Random-access memory

The player's memory holds the software used to run the title or application, and a few features like soundmaps (small blocks of sound that are used repeatedly in a programme) and sprites (small repeatedly used visual images, such as an unusual cursor). It is also used to hold video images and graphics. It is divided into two areas, each of half a megabyte, called picture planes. The picture planes are used to manipulate images – for example, to dissolve from an image on one plane to an image on another.

Full-motion video decoder

Processing is more complicated for full-motion video than for still images, so the CD-I player has a special dedicated microchip and half a megabyte of memory. If this subsystem is not used for full-motion video, it can be used for other purposes. Full-motion pictures play on a third picture plane in addition to the two mentioned above.

The anatomy of the disc

The disc looks the same as a normal CD audio disc. Everything on it, whether video, audio or control software, is held as digital

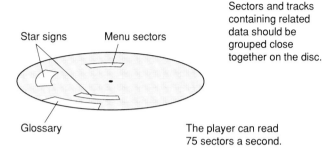

The disc is laid out in tracks made up of sectors. Each sector contains data of one type: video, audio, text or control.

Star signs   Menu sectors

Glossary

Sectors and tracks containing related data should be grouped close together on the disc.

The player can read 75 sectors a second.

Figure 4.3 The arrangement of sectors on a disc.

information or data. The data – up to 650 megabytes of it – is laid out on the disc in **tracks** that contain individual **sectors** of around two kilobytes each.

The tracks are arranged in a long spiral. The player can play data from any part of the disc. The farther apart pieces of data are on the disc, the longer it takes to move between them – up to two or three seconds. For this reason, the way the data is mapped out on the disc is important (Figure 4.3). During production the disc layout must be optimized so that it is as efficient as possible. Figure 4.4 contains some facts and figures about what the disc holds.

Sectors and tracks

The CD-I disc can hold a maximum of 99 tracks, each of which must be at least four seconds long. The area of the disc that holds these tracks is known as the programme area. There are two sorts of track:

- data tracks contain control software and other data
- audio tracks contain only CD-DA data

Each track is made up of a variable number of sectors, each containing 2352 bytes of data. There are five types of sector:

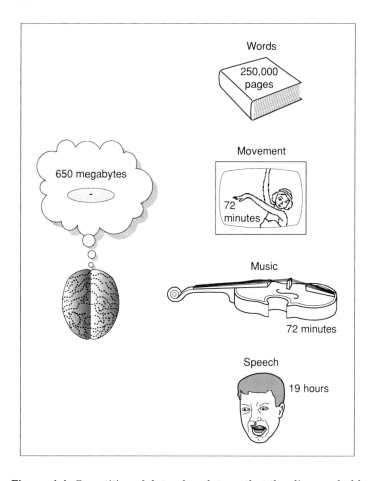

Figure 4.4 Quantities of data of each type that the disc can hold.

- audio: contains audio data
- video: contains video data
- data: contains control software and other data
- empty: used to fill up file space, particularly in real-time files
- message: used to warn people playing CD-I discs on ordinary CD-DA players to lower the volume on the player and advance to the next track

Each sector has a **header**, an area carrying information about what sort of data the sector contains, whether or not it is real-

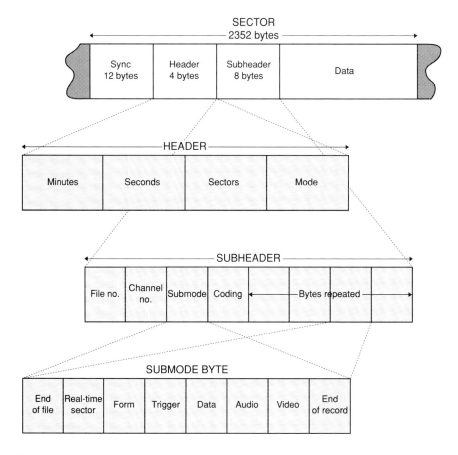

Figure 4.5 The CD-I sector. Its type is specified in the so-called submode byte.

time, and which channel(s) it is to use (Figure 4.5). A sector can contain only the type of data defined by its header. It is impossible and unnecessary to combine information of different types in a single sector. The arrangement of different types of sector is important: see the sections below on synchronization and interleaving.

The information in the header is read by the player's operating system (CD-RTOS). The operating system acts like a signal box on the railways; it directs the data in the sector to the appropriate part of the player. For example, data from an audio sector would pass through the ADPCM decoder, and then to the speakers.

From disc to player

Data rate or bandwidth

The process of playing the CD-I disc involves reading the data from the disc and routing it through the appropriate channel to the part of the player that will decode it before playing it. The rate at which data is transferred is called the **data rate** or **bandwidth**.

The maximum rate at which data can be transferred is 172 kilobytes per second. This is one of the controlling factors in CD-I production. You cannot produce any effects that demand more data than this to be read from the disc at any one time.

Channels

The data passes from the disc through the player to the screen or speakers through a number of channels. This is exactly like a river breaking up into separate streams. In many cases, such as high-quality audio signals, a single piece of material may use more than one channel. There are 32 channels in total.

Channels are the neck of the funnel through which the data is poured. You can use up to 16 channels to transfer audio data. Higher-quality sound requires more data, and so uses more channels. For example, Level A stereo-quality sound takes up all 16 sound channels. But Level C mono sound takes up only one channel. So you can have up to 16 parallel sound tracks for a particular scene if you use Level C mono, but only one if you use Level A stereo.

Seek time

Seek time is the time taken by the playing head to move from one part of the disc to another. The maximum time allowed by the Green Book specification is three seconds from the edge of the disc to the centre (or vice versa). If the disc head has to read widely separated data, there should not be a gap of more than three seconds.

CD-I design can overcome this in several ways: firstly, by interleaving data so that, as far as possible, pieces of data relating to the same part of the title are in the same place; secondly, by laying out the disc in such a way that the related bits of data are never far away from each other – in other words, the geography of the disc should reflect the structure of the programme; lastly, by accepting that there are bound to be some slight delays while the player reads and processes data, and treating them dynamically. A maximum of three seconds is not very long anyway, and can easily be disguised by, for instance, a tune or a lively graphic stored in the player's memory. It can even be turned into a positive feature of the programme.

Synchronization

Getting all the media to work together is slightly more complicated in CD-I than in other media. For example, on videotape the soundtrack runs alongside the pictures, so they are automatically synchronized. However, as we have seen, on the CD-I disc audio, video and software sectors are held separately, so the information that ensures they are played together is held in the header record of each sector.

The advantage of this is that the same asset can be synchronized in different ways. For example, if it is accompanying a German commentary a picture might need to occur at a different time to when it is accompanying a commentary in another language, because German takes longer to say things than many other languages.

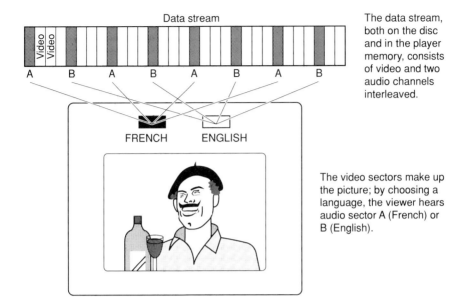

The data stream, both on the disc and in the player memory, consists of video and two audio channels interleaved.

The video sectors make up the picture; by choosing a language, the viewer hears audio sector A (French) or B (English).

Figure 4.6 Interleaving is the alternation in the data stream of information relating to different video pictures and audio tracks, which are simultaneously available to the viewer.

Interleaving

All the data required to produce a particular scene should be kept in neighbouring sectors on the disc. Because a picture often uses more sectors than a soundtrack, it might be necessary to have four sectors containing video data for every one containing audio and every one containing software data. Placing them together makes a pattern in the track, as seen in Figure 4.6. Interleaving can be used to store parallel soundtracks or video tracks.

Real time

Real time is the time in which everyone lives. CD-I is 'real-time' because it responds instantly to the commands of those who are using it in one way or another. It also means that the data plays as it is read off the disc. So if an image is to be displayed for a certain length of time after the data for the image has been read and displayed, a number of empty sectors must be put on the disc to take up the required time.

The basis of this real-time capacity is CD-RTOS, the Compact Disc Real-Time Operating System. Unlike the operating systems of many personal computers it is multitasking, which means it can deal with more than one problem at a time. Real-time operation and multitasking are essential to the interactive capacity of CD-I. When the viewer interacts or reacts, the system must be able to respond instantly and in real time.

Real-time files must be synchronized with the other contents of CD-I sectors. In the header section of any sector a bit (the smallest possible unit of computer data) can be enabled, or 'switched on', to indicate that the sector is real-time. In general, sectors that serve some real-time CD-I function will have the real-time bit set, while those containing (for example) applications software will not.

Optional extras

All CD-I players include a pointing device for moving the cursor around the screen and selecting items from menus. CD-I players come with either a remote control (the home version, Figure 4.7(a)) or a mouse (the professional version). The basic configuration of the CD-I player is specified in the Green Book but it has the capacity to expand and change in some ways. This reflects the fact that designs for CD-I will come in all shapes and

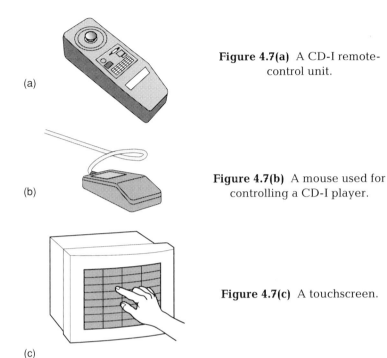

(a)

Figure 4.7(a) A CD-I remote-control unit.

(b)

Figure 4.7(b) A mouse used for controlling a CD-I player.

Figure 4.7(c) A touchscreen.

(c)

sizes. Apart from mainstream designs for the mass market, there are likely to be specialist applications that require different things of the player and need different gadgets and peripherals to work. The designer's choice of controlling device will be governed by what the audience is likely to have, and how and where they will use the programme.

Mouse

A mouse (Figure 4.7(b)) may be used to provide more precise control over the pointer on the screen – for example, in titles with more than the usual half a dozen menu choices on a screen, in professional applications where the player is sited on a desk, or in simulation titles that demand close control.

Joystick

For games and simulations, a joystick offers more control than the standard remote-control unit.

Touchscreen

A touchscreen (Figure 4.7(c)) offers a simpler and more immediate way of selecting items from a display. This is a particularly appropriate device for point-of-sale and point-of-information applications.

Keyboard

Although CD-I is a read-only device – that is, you cannot input large amounts of information – a keyboard allows a more sophisticated level of response to programmes. This might be ideal for education or training applications in which the user types in answers to questions.

Non-volatile memory

Some programmes will exploit the player's non-volatile or permanent memory, in which a small amount of information specific to the user can be stored for use by programmes and retained between sessions. When the player is switched off the data is not lost. This means that, for example, sophisticated and detailed user profiles can be built up and kept, more games scores can be retained and other programming tricks become possible. The player has up to eight kilobytes of non-volatile memory.

Diskette drive

A computer-style diskette drive might be used to offload information, results, data and responses. Professional players often have a slot for adding extra memory. With a keyboard and additional memory, sophisticated applications combining computer programs with CD-I titles could be developed, extending the CD-I experience into new markets.

Video input

The back picture plane (see page 50), when it is not being used for motion video by a CD-I title, can be used to display video from an external analogue source. This allows the superimposition of CD-I programme images upon a video input. Thus real-time CD-I notes could accompany a video film, for example, or faces in CD-I records could be compared with the live video image of a person for security purposes.

Conclusion

An understanding of the basics of CD-I technology is essential both for production managers and for the production and technical staff implementing the design. It is especially important to understand what CD-I equipment the audience for the programme is likely to have, and what, if any, needs to be supplied with the programme.

Take the example of a training CD-I on company procedures, produced for a major multinational corporation new to the medium. The client will want to know how much each CD-I workstation is going to cost, and may set a limit on the amount. The programme designers will need to be briefed accordingly, so that they don't come up with a programme that requires lots of extra devices. Several soundtracks will be required to cover all the languages used; fitting these onto the same disc in parallel will reduce mastering and pressing costs, but will also have an impact on the amount of non-audio data that can be used.

Working out all these factors before detailed design of the programme begins will help designers and producers to get the best out of CD-I, and help clients get the result they want.

5

CD-I effects

Introduction

We have looked at the player and the disc. Now we survey some of the effects available using these resources. The effects fall into two categories: video and audio. This survey is intended as a brief outline from the production point of view. For a fuller description, see *The CD-I Design Handbook*.

Picture planes

The visual effects available on the CD-I centre around the idea of picture planes (Figure 5.1). There are four planes:

- the back plane is reserved for full-motion video
- the next two planes are used for all other visual effects
- the front plane is used for the cursor

Imagine each plane having the capacity to act both as a full or as a partial window to the plane behind it, and as a cinema screen upon which images of some type are displayed. The play

A and B are used for most
purposes – pictures, graphics,
text, menus etc. Each uses up to
half a megabyte of the player memory.

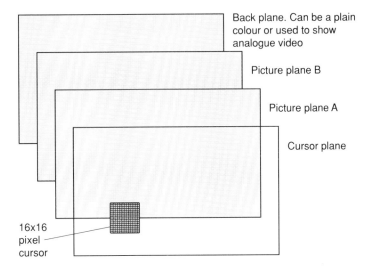

Back plane. Can be a plain
colour or used to show
analogue video

Picture plane B

Picture plane A

Cursor plane

16x16
pixel
cursor

Figure 5.1 Picture planes.

of images between the planes can be a dynamic one. A variety
of cuts and wipes between planes is available. The order of the
planes (A in front of B, or B in front of A and so on) is set from the
display control program.

When and how...

*The ordering of images on planes takes place at the authoring
stage. If you are using a high-level authoring system, you will not
have much say about what goes on what plane: the authoring
system takes care of that for you. However, if you are working at
the deeper level you will be able to determine what goes where.*

Image types

You can use a variety of different types of image, which are usually encoded in different ways. Some ways of encoding an image digitally suit certain types of image better than others. For example, the best method of encoding graphic text is not the best method of encoding colour photographs.

In the section that follows, image types are often referred to by their initials or short names. If you are unfamiliar with these, you will find a brief description in the Glossary at the end of the book. There is more detailed information on encoding images in Chapter 6.

Full-motion video (FMV)

Moving natural images taking up the whole screen, of quality at least comparable to VHS.

Partial-motion video

Two types of partial-motion/partial-screen video are available. They can run on any of the picture planes except the cursor plane.

Partial motion consists of moving pictures with less than 20 frames per second, and is good for 'how to...' sequences, surrogate walk-throughs and so on.

Using a *partial screen* for motion takes up less bandwidth and memory than the full screen at the normal frame rate. If you use only half the screen for motion video, you use only half as much memory and half as much storage space on the disc.

RGB

Good for high-quality colour pictures – for example, works of art.

DYUV

For good-quality natural images, such as colour photographs.

Colour Look-Up Table (CLUT)

Suits less complex natural images. Images are compressed by referring to a colour look-up table, rather than storing the absolute colour value of each pixel. Several forms of CLUT are available, using different numbers of colours and hence requiring more or less storage space. For example, the eight-bit CLUT 8 format is suitable for simple natural images and allows up to 256 colours to be used. CLUT 3 allows a smaller number of colours to be used, but takes up less space and is ideal for images that form part of an animation that will then be run-length encoded (see below).

The versatility of CLUTs is extended by their capacity to change palettes during the display of an image, so that more than the theoretical CLUT 8 maximum of 256 colours can be used in a single screen image. This is explained in more detail below.

Run-length encoding (RLE)

A technique for compressing the amount of code needed to store a colour image. RLE does not suit natural images, but is excellent for text, graphics and simple animation.

QHY (Quantized High-Y)

A very high-quality natural image type that is produced by using a source to generate both a high-resolution RGB image and a separate, normal-resolution image. The differences between them are analysed, to give detailed information on the luminance changes between the two images. These differences are then encoded via RLE (above).

QHY is efficient in terms of data storage and produces a high-quality image; however, it can be used only on CD-I players equipped with optional high-resolution screens. So before QHY is used as an image format by your programme designers, you should make sure that your client expects the audience for your programme to have that level of equipment.

> **When and how...**
>
> *It is important to decide during the design phase what quality will be needed for each image and to ensure that images are grabbed and encoded at the highest-possible quality level. As an insurance, many designers use batch processing to convert each image to a range of formats and coding types, in case changes need to be made during the design process.*
>
> *Motion video for CD-I is encoded after the video film has been made and edited but before authoring (post-production) has started.*
>
> *Static images are either developed as digital (RGB) images or converted from analogue sources. From there they can be converted into any of the other image types. Although the designer should have a good idea of what image type is to be used in what context, final decisions can be made in the authoring process according to criteria such as space available on the disc and image quality required.*

Broadcasting conventions

The decision about which national markets the CD-I is aimed at is an important one because its effects extend even to the way in which images are encoded. Different countries broadcast television pictures using different numbers of lines. The three main television broadcasting conventions are:

- PAL: Britain, Europe except France, Australia, Africa, South America; 625 lines
- NTSC: North America and Japan; 525 lines
- SECAM: France; 625 lines

The screen sizes in CD-I are measured in pixels. The number of lines in the screen affects the number of pixels required to make a CD-I picture that will play on it. The screen sizes are:

NTSC	PAL/SECAM
360 × 240	384 × 280

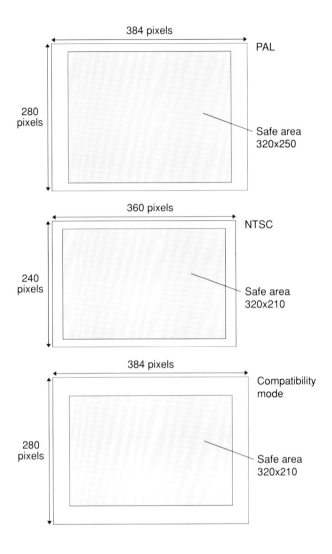

Figure 5.2 PAL, NTSC and compatibility modes, with
their corresponding safe areas.

Ideally, CD-I programmes should be playable on any player
anywhere in the world. This can be done easily; a CD-I made for
NTSC markets can be played on a PAL television set and a PAL
CD-I can be played on an NTSC television. The player automatically cuts off the edge of an image that is too big, or adds a

> **When and how...**
>
> The decision about what broadcasting standard the production is being developed for should have been made at the beginning of the design process. It will emerge from discussions about the audience, market and concept for the CD-I. SECAM sets are treated as PAL.

blank area around the edge of the image to fill up the screen if it is too small, and then centres the image. But if you want to ensure that the pictures really work properly on any type of television, you should use compatibility mode (see Figure 5.2).

An additional factor to be taken into consideration is that video pictures tend to drift beyond the edge of the visible screen. Because of this, for each broadcasting standard there is a 'safety area'. This is the area of the screen inside which you should put parts of the picture, such as hotspots, that you do not want to risk getting lost beyond the edge of the visible screen. The safety areas for each broadcasting convention are:

NTSC	PAL/SECAM
320×210 pixels	320×250 pixels

To work in compatibility mode, you must assume the larger screen size (that is, PAL) and the smaller safety area (that is, NTSC). Thus compatibility mode has these pixel dimensions:

screen size	384×280 pixels
safety area	320×210 pixels

Resolution

The resolution of a picture is defined as the number of pixels used to make it. This varies according to the number of lines making up the television picture. The two standards are 525 lines and 625 lines.

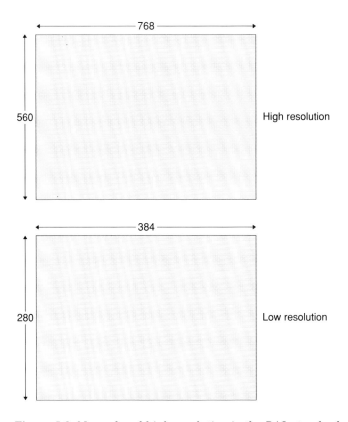

Figure 5.3 Normal and high resolution in the PAL standard.

There are three resolution levels in CD-I. For the most part only normal resolution will be used. Double resolution doubles the number of pixels in the width of the picture, while high resolution doubles the number of pixels in the height and width (Table 5.1 and Figure 5.3). Most images are converted into RGB or developed in RGB high-resolution format.

Table 5.1 Screen resolution in pixels for different broadcasting standards.

Resolution	Standard	
	NTSC	PAL/SECAM
Normal	360 × 240	384 × 280
Double	720 × 240	768 × 280
High	720 × 480	768 × 560 (interlaced)

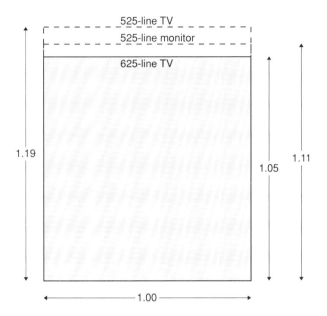

Figure 5.4 Aspect ratio in the 525- and 625-line systems. It is defined as pixel height/pixel width.

Aspect ratios

When a PAL picture is shown on an NTSC television set (or vice versa), the slightly different shape of the screen means that the shape of the pixels composing the picture is distorted. For example, because the PAL picture is slightly squarer than the NTSC picture, a shape that appears perfectly circular on the PAL set would be squashed and elongated on the NTSC set (Figure 5.4).

The proportion of width to height of an individual pixel is known as its aspect ratio. If you want to avoid any distortion of the aspect ratio, then you should create and author the title directly for the system that it is going to be played on. However, research has proved that viewers can tolerate up to 10% distortion in the aspect ratio of a figure on their screens before it starts to disturb them. If you use compatibility mode, distortion when played on either system is kept within this limit.

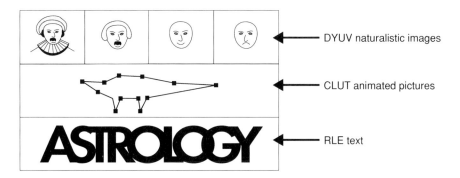

DYUV naturalistic images

CLUT animated pictures

RLE text

Figure 5.5 Using different compression types in one image. Each picture plane can be divided into horizontal bands, called subscreens, using different compression types.

The distortion figures for aspect ratios when you transfer a production from one broadcasting convention to another are given in Table 5.2.

Table 5.2 Percentage distortion of aspect ratio for each format when displayed on the three target systems.

Display of target system	525-line monitor	525-line TV	625-line
Format			
525-line	0	+7.0	– 6.0
625-line	+6.0	+13.0	0
Compatible	+3.0	+10.0	– 3.0

Subscreens

An image plane can be divided up into any number of subscreens, which may contain images of different coding types and/or resolution. For example, in a quiz you might want to display a DYUV natural image, such as a photograph of a singer, and use a less space- and bandwidth-consuming format such as a CLUT or RLE for the text of the questions underneath the image (Figure 5.5).

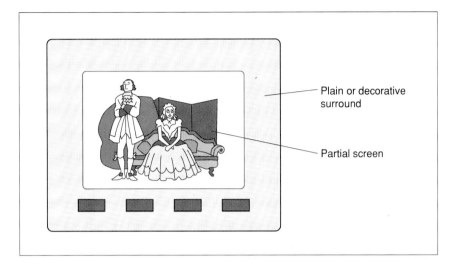

Figure 5.6 Partial-screen motion. A partial-screen video picture uses proportionately less memory than the whole screen would, and can be just as effective.

When and how...

Subscreens are not available at the simplest level of authoring, but they are used with more sophisticated authoring software, such as Philips' Balboa Runtime Environment, described on page 121. Subscreens are useful if you have a DYUV image but want CLUT 7 text at the bottom.

Partial updates

Partial updates display fresh images that are smaller than the whole area of the screen. They are partial because only a defined area of an image on one picture plane is being updated, and not the whole image (Figure 5.6).

The area of the image that is updated can be rectangular or irregular. With rectangular partial updates, the new partial image is coded as a normal image of reduced size, and inserted into the main image at a place specified by coordinates. Irregular partial updates are coded by giving the start position and the length of each line of the image.

When DYUV images are partially updated, there has to be a small transition area between the larger image and the area that is being partially updated. This is because DYUV images are encoded by recording the difference between neighbouring pixels in a row. The transition area at the beginning and end of each line of the partial image is to allow the change between its colour and brightness values and those of the surrounding image.

You can use partial updates to create motion in a small area of the screen. For example, an animated figure could be introduced into an image as a partial update.

When and how...

Partial updates have to be programmed at the authoring stage, using sophisticated authoring tools. Rectangular partial updates are easier to program than irregular ones.

CLUT animation

A CLUT is a Colour Look-Up Table. It consists of a large number of colours arranged in table form and held in the player's memory. When a picture is displayed, instead of having to process the code for the red, green and blue values of every pixel, the player only has to refer to the position of the colour in the look-up table (Figure 5.7).

One way to achieve simple animation effects is to change the colours in the look-up table. So, while the code for the image remains the same, a rapid change in the contents of the CLUT

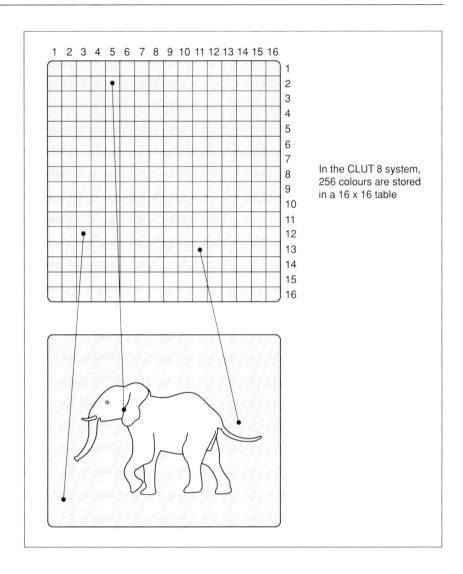

1 2 3 4 5 6 7 8 9 10 11 12 13 14 15 16

In the CLUT 8 system, 256 colours are stored in a 16 x 16 table

Figure 5.7 Image compression: Colour Look Up Table (CLUT). When an image is displayed, the colour of each pixel is not given an absolute value. Instead its position in the colour table is specified.

means that parts of the image can be flashing on and off and changing colour, as in pictures of people winking and stars twinkling.

Dynamic updates

Dynamic updates are used to increase the number of colours available. Eight CLUT locations (in effect eight colours) can be changed in each line at any one time. This means that, instead of the 256 colours available in the look-up table for CLUT 8 images, you can have eight new colours for every line of the display.

This can be used to give the effect of a larger colour palette. Two or more partial screens can be used, each with a different CLUT. This kind of effect is useful for twinkling images and for vertical shading, such as sunset skies (Figure 5.8).

Sprites

Sprites are little blocks of video data that can be stored in the memory of the player. They can be accessed from there at any point in the program, which means that they are suitable for functions such as more elaborate types of cursor, or effects used to enliven the screen when there are intervals of seek time.

Scrolling

Images larger than the full screen dimensions can be encoded and loaded by the player. That is, although the code for the whole picture is sitting in the CD-I player's memory, only a part of it is being displayed on the screen. A scrolling effect is achieved in CD-I by moving the area that is to be displayed across the area of the larger image, like the viewfinder of a camera (Figure 5.9). The movement of the window can be horizontal, vertical or a combination of the two.

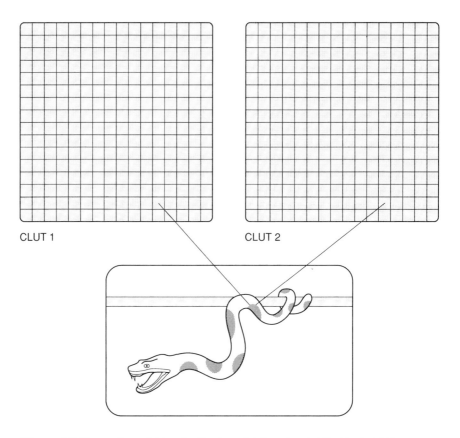

CLUT 1   CLUT 2

Figure 5.8 Dynamic updating. In the time it takes the dot that 'paints' the screen to go from the end of one frame to the start of the next, a new CLUT can be loaded. Changing CLUTs permits a wider range of colours to be employed. Also, a given pixel can be assigned a different colour without changing its CLUT number, which is useful for some animation effects. Thus the colours of this snake can shimmer as the CLUT tables are alternated.

Video-plane effects

Transparency

Any pixel on any plane can be coded to make it transparent, so that images on the plane behind it can be seen. Full-motion

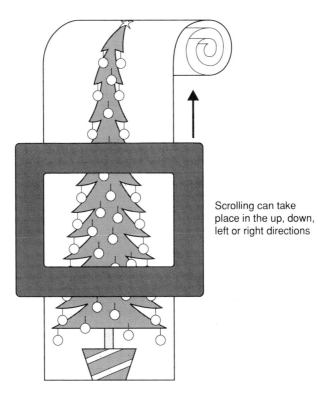

Scrolling can take
place in the up, down,
left or right directions

Figure 5.9 When the picture is scrolled, the screen acts
as a window onto a larger image that is moved past it.

video (FMV), for instance, requires that the front two planes be
transparent, so that the viewer can see the FMV on the back
plane – unless you want to use the front planes for overlay
effects produced with an authoring system (Figure 5.10).

There are two ways of making images transparent, which
may be used individually or in combination on the two image
planes:

- mattes – used to make transparent areas on one plane
  through which the plane behind it can be seen

- chroma key – makes all areas of a certain colour on one plane
  transparent, so that areas on the plane behind it can be seen

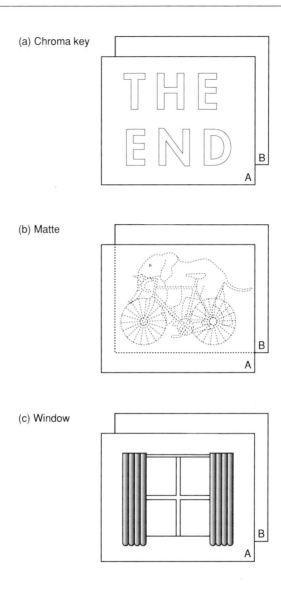

(a) Chroma key

(b) Matte

(c) Window

Figure 5.10 Transparency effects. (a) Chroma key. The letters on plane A were originally green. Green pixels are selectively made transparent to show some of plane B. (b) Matte. The pixels of the image on the front plane become transparent to achieve a dissolve from the front to the back image. (c) Window. The selected window area on the front plane is made transparent to show some of the moving image on the back plane.

> **When and how...**
> *Manipulation of mattes and chroma key takes place at the authoring stage. At present the simpler high-level authoring packages cannot cope with this effect.*

Fades and dissolves

Fade-up and fade-down are increase and decrease in the brightness of an image. A fade is a gentle way of starting or ending a sequence of images. A dissolve is the simultaneous fade-down of one image and fade-up of another to provide a smooth transition between two images. With FMV, fades and dissolves have to be implemented before the material is encoded.

> **When and how...**
> *Fades and dissolves are engineered at the authoring stage. Most authoring packages already cope with the relatively uncomplicated coding requirements without any fuss.*

Mosaics

Mosaics break down images and produce effects such as:

- granulation
- magnification or zoom
- low-resolution images

They work by manipulating the pixels that make up the image. **Pixel hold** takes a pixel and holds its value until the next pixel after some fixed interval is encountered (Figure 5.11). For example, if it is working on every third pixel, the value of every

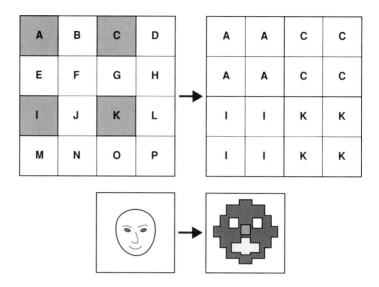

Figure 5.11 Pixel hold. The image is kept the same size while the definition is coarsened. This can be repeated to dissolve the image into large coloured squares.

third pixel is held and the values in between are forgotten. **Pixel repeat** duplicates pixels to produce magnification effects. It simply repeats each pixel a set number of times (Figure 5.12).

Cuts and wipes

The most basic items in a film-maker's vocabulary are cuts and wipes. They are the means of passing from one scene or image to the next. CD-I offers a number of devices based on cuts and wipes as a standard part of its armoury. They are divided into one- and two-plane effects. They are not the only ones you can use – others can be invented. However, for the time being these are the most commonly available ones, since even high-level authoring programs will cope with them. Typically, a cut moves quickly from one image to the next, while a wipe involves a transitional period in which a part of both images is visible. For example, the image on the front image plane may part in the centre like a pair of curtains, to reveal the image on the plane behind it.

> **When and how...**
> A standard set of cuts and wipes is available in the most basic authoring systems. New varieties will doubtless become available in high-level authoring packages, while if you have a really novel idea, you may require programmers to write the software routine that powers it.

Table 5.3 Summary of visual CD-I effects.

Effect	Description	One/two planes
Cut	One image is immediately substituted for another	
Fade-up/ down	An image progressively brightens or darkens	1
Dissolve	One image progressively replaced by another	2
Pixel repeat	A part of an image is magnified by repeating each pixel a set number of times	1
Pixel hold	Coarsening the definition of an image by repeating pixels at fixed intervals and obliterating their neighbours	1
Scrolling	Moving the window to be displayed on the screen across a larger image that is stored in the player's memory	1
Partial update	Updating only a part of the total screen area	1
Wipe	The progressive replacement of one image by another. The ways in which an image on one plane can give way to an image on the other include curtain, blind and square.	2
Transparency	Making areas in one plane through which areas on the other plane can be viewed. Transparency can be chroma key (areas of a particular colour become transparent) or matte (shaped areas become transparent).	2

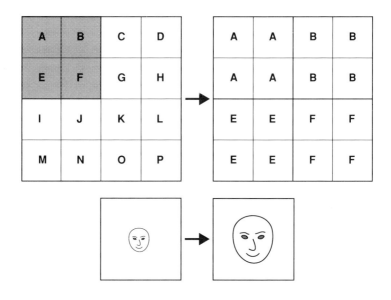

Figure 5.12 Pixel repeat. The image is enlarged, with a consequent coarsening.

Audio

Like video, audio can be used at various qualities on a CD-I. In addition to ordinary audio compact-disc quality, there are three other CD-I quality levels. Each of the three can be either mono or stereo.

Although it is tempting always to use the highest-quality sound, you should remember that the higher sound qualities use more disc space. They also use up more of the data stream on their way from the disc to the speakers. So higher quality may not only be frankly unnecessary – for example, for speech – but also use valuable data storage space and limit the number of things you can have going on at the same time in the production.

Sound quality formats

For the very highest-quality sound use CD-DA. This is the quality used on CD audio discs. You would be unlikely to require such high-quality sound for a normal CD-I production, although if you were making a CD-I Ready disc, which is essentially a sound recording plus some electronic sleeve notes, you might use it.

For slightly less hi-fi sound, use Level A. This is equivalent to the sort of sound quality you get when you play a new LP on good-quality equipment, although without any of the background wow and flutter. Level A stereo takes up 50% of the data stream, leaving the other 50% for video, graphics, text and so on. Level A mono takes up only 25%. You can get two hours of stereo or four hours of mono Level A sound on a CD-I disc.

Level B sound is equivalent to a first-class FM radio broadcast, and it takes up 25% of the data stream. You can get up to four hours of stereo Level B sound on a CD-I disc.

Level C is more like AM radio received under good conditions. It is completely adequate for speech. It occupies 6% of the data stream, leaving 94% for other things. You can get about 19 hours of Level C mono on a CD-I disc.

Soundmaps

Reading data from the disc is not the only method of playing sound on CD-I. Small blocks of data can be stored in the memory of the player, where they are quickly accessible.

Soundmaps are suitable for producing repeated sound effects, such as tunes and other sounds that accompany menu choices and let the viewer know that their choice has been registered by the programme, or bursts of applause that reinforce the player's correct selection in a quiz.

Effects and production decisions

Choices about what sort of effect will be used where should already have been made by the CD-I designer. The detailed design specification will have had to consider these issues in order to see how much space the program will take on the disc, and whether the data flow is within the capacity of the CD-I player. However, it may be that later adjustments to the detailed specification have to be made. Making these is the responsibility of the producer, although the whole team will also be involved.

For this reason it is advisable to keep materials in a form in which they are available for reuse. For example, you should keep audio resources in their original PCM (pulse-code modulated) form. If you then find that you can't use a Level A stereo version of the resource, you can go back and make a Level B version, or whatever sound quality you require.

Similarly, because converting artwork and graphics into CLUT or DYUV formats is usually a batch operation, it may be easier and cheaper to convert them all into both formats at the outset, so you can juggle space on the disc if necessary without having to go back and reconvert materials.

Producers should also be aware of the types of video effects that are available so that they can accurately assess the suitability of different authoring and production environments for the planned programme. A highly visual CD-I programme with a great many complex special effects will need more complex production facilities and authoring software than a simple programme with straightforward cuts and wipes.

Designers should be made aware of the possible limitations of the environment in which a programme must be developed and produced, and if necessary more expensive facilities and new authoring or graphic design software will have to be budgeted for.

Conclusion

CD-I offers a rich environment that programme designers can exploit to produce visually exciting productions, with a higher-quality soundtrack than most television viewers will have experienced. However, both designers and producers need to pick their way through all the choices in both sound and image formats to ensure that they can produce their intended programme within the technical constraints of the CD-I player and disc and the financial constraints of their budget.

6

Gathering and converting materials

Introduction

There is nothing to stop you making your CD-I production in the same way as any other: that is, filming and sound-recording using analogue media, generating artwork through conventional methods, and then going through the process of converting it all into digital files later on. However, given the digital nature of CD-I, it makes sense to take account of its particular requirements from the outset and minimize the effort and time involved in digital conversion.

Of course, this may not always be possible. When you are using existing materials, such as promotional films, slides, artwork or music, they are unlikely to have been created with an eye to future CD-I productions and will not be in a suitable form for you to take files of data and start editing them for use in the CD-I.

This chapter discusses the coding methods underlying the storage of materials in digital form on CD-I discs, how to generate the right sort of materials from scratch and to convert existing materials from non-CD-I formats, and how to manipulate and edit materials at different levels of authoring sophistication.

Gathering, converting and editing material are probably the most labour-intensive stages of CD-I and will involve technical staff from various disciplines working together to assemble materials that match the detailed design specification.

CD-I and video

Pictures in CD-I fall into two main categories. The first consists of a broad range of visual material, from animated sequences to still natural images and graphics. The second is motion video. Motion-video natural images have their own special subsystem on the CD-I player and are encoded differently from other types of video material.

Motion-video encoding

Video on CD-I has to be handled carefully. Although picture quality is high (as good as Super VHS video) there are still a number of restrictions. Very fast movement and the movement of sharply contrasting objects against each other (for example, a bouncing ping-pong ball) can produce coloured ghost images as the encoding catches up with the picture. A large amount of full-screen full-motion video (FMV) in a production uses up a lot of data storage space, and so reduces the possibility of doing other things.

To code a single frame of a television-type moving image takes a megabyte of memory unless compression techniques are used. Compression techniques are ways of reducing the number of binary digits it takes to store images or sounds, and hence the space occupied by the stored image on disc and in memory. Displaying full-motion video of natural moving images at 25 frames per second requires considerable technical sleight of hand, since only 172 kilobytes per second can be transferred through the CD-I system.

Video footage should be shot in the normal way, using standard video-recording equipment, and processed afterwards for use in CD-I. Typically this would involve going out with a shooting script and a video crew, although the amount of money available for producing new video footage for inclusion in the programme may extend to a much more sophisticated set-up. It may be as well to bear in mind the strengths and weaknesses of full-motion video on CD-I when shooting video footage.

Motion-video encoding

Strengths	Weaknesses
Good definition	Not good for sharp colour or tone contrasts
Digital image can be manipulated in various ways	Not good for sudden or rapid movements

---

Many CD-I producers will be working with existing film and video recordings shot for use in other media, such as film, television and video, and this material will need to be examined for its suitability for inclusion in CD-I programmes. For example, in one edition of a game show the hostess may be wearing a dress that is less vibrant than usual, and works better when converted to CD-I.

Existing footage will, of course, need to be checked for possible continuity problems. If it is impossible to ensure complete consistency throughout the programme, it should be possible at least to make sure that performers are dressed and made up consistently for each module or section of the planned programme.

Older material will need to be checked to ensure that it is up to date – a glossy training programme will look less good, for example, if it features an out-of-date version of the company name or sign on the inevitable shot of the company headquarters.

The videotape is run through a frame-grabber. This converts each frame of the moving image into digital format. Frame-grabbers work at various quality levels, labelled from D1 to D3.

Video formats

VHS	Betacam
VHS-S	Betacam Super plus
U-Matic $\frac{3}{4}$"	1" C format
Hi Band U-Matic $\frac{3}{4}$"	

It is pointless to use the very highest-quality (D3) frame-grabber to digitize pictures, because it produces more detail than CD-I needs or can cope with.

Once the videotape has been digitized, it can be encoded. This can be a lengthy process, since each frame can take many seconds to deal with, although not every frame is directly encoded.

Encoding takes sequences of between three and six frames, looks at the first and last pictures in each sequence, and encodes the differences between them. This means that the full digital code is not kept for every single frame but only for the frames at the beginning and end of each sequence, thus saving a considerable amount of data storage space. In effect, the decoding routine that takes place in the player when the title is played makes informed guesses about what happens in the frames in between the first and last frames of each sequence. So long as things don't change too fast, these guesses are usually adequate to give the appearance of natural and smooth motion.

The production sequence

Activity	Format
Filming	Betacam tape
Off-line edit	VHS tape
On-line edit	Edited Betacam
Digitization	Digital files in YUV format
FMV encoding	FMV files

The less movement there is in a sequence (and the more even and predictable that movement) the more frames can simply be encoded as differences. So, in a slow sequence, every sixth frame might be used for encoding differences, whereas in a fast sequence, every third frame would be more appropriate.

Full-motion video can be encoded all at one rate, or at a variable rate. Obviously, if the second option is adopted more attention has to be paid to the process; the encoding machine cannot simply be switched on and left to get on with it – it must be told when to change (for example) from six frames to three frames.

When playing CD-I FMV, you cannot do a freeze-frame without moving to the nearest full frame of video, nor can you play a sequence backwards. This effect can only be created as a simulation: you would, in effect, have to code the videotape backwards as well as forwards, so the audience would be looking at a separately coded sequence when they thought they were playing the film backwards.

The places at which you can stop or start the motion picture are known as entry points. At these points in the data on the disc, all the code to make a complete picture is present. You can have an entry point up to every two seconds throughout any full-motion video sequence.

Editing and manipulating full-motion video images

Editing full-motion video images can take place either before or after they are digitized.

The arguments for editing the videotape before it is digitized are that it is cheaper and it does not tie up expensive and specialized equipment.

The arguments against are that you might not be able to do all the things you need to do when editing the videotape, and it is difficult to be as precise as you may want to be. For example, you might not be able to specify that the motion sequence is going to appear in a certain window on the screen. It is also more difficult to cut sequences to precisely the length that may be demanded by the matching slot in your CD-I programme design.

The answer may be to do an edit list on paper, and then transfer the Betacam tape video to VHS tape, using cheap video equipment. Next, the Betacam tape can be edited on-line before sending the whole thing to be digitized and encoded. The rest of the editing may then take place at the CD-I-specific part of post-production, as part of the authoring process.

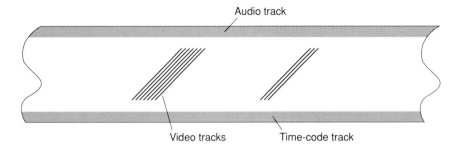

Figure 6.1 Video and audio tracks on a videotape.

Sound and full-motion video

The treatment of sound in the editing process is more complicated. When lipsynch is involved, timing has to be accurate to
$\frac{1}{20}$th of a second, or a difference between sound and picture is
noticeable.

On a videotape, the time code and the audio track are
automatically synchronized with the corresponding video frames
simply by being positioned at each side of them (Figure 6.1).
When the tape is digitized, the audio and video are separated.
The audio is digitized into audio files, and the video into video
files. At the same time, the time codes from the videotape are
encoded in both files, to ensure that synchronization is possible.

The start, stop and entry points of FMV sequences each
contain the time-code addresses from the videotape. The time
code is one of the pieces of data that is held in the header of each
FMV sector, as it is also held in the header for the matching
audio sectors (Figure 6.2). This makes it possible for the sound
to synchronize exactly with the correct frame or sequence.

The sound and picture are brought together again during the
authoring process, when they are interleaved on the disc.
Subsequently, when the program plays, pictures and sounds
are perfectly synchronized.

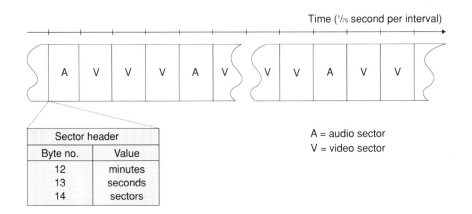

Figure 6.2 table:

Sector header	
Byte no.	Value
12	minutes
13	seconds
14	sectors

A = audio sector
V = video sector

Figure 6.2 CD-I track, showing audio and video sectors in a motion-video real-time file. Headers synchronize audio and video.

Stills and graphics

Using still images and graphics

Still pictures and graphics are likely to make up the substance of many CD-I productions. Provided you make sure that you end up with the appropriate type of file, there are very few restrictions on what you can and can't use. Depending on the availability of equipment, you may be able to carry out parts of the process of creating images in-house, or you may have to go to outside studios for all or part of the process.

Capturing natural images and camera-ready artwork

A natural image can be anything from an existing photograph to a physical object, from a slide image to a frame from a moving film. Camera-ready artwork is the final version of work created by graphic or other artists.

Before a graphic can be converted to any of the various image types, it must initially be in the RGB digital format. This is a technique for scanning images and storing data about each part of them. Images are initially captured in high-resolution format. 'RGB' stands for 'Red Green Blue'; in RGB 888 eight data bits are used for storing details of each colour, while in RGB 555 the corresponding number of bits is five. The RGB image is converted to IFF (Interchange File Format) and finally formatted into any of the standard CD-I image types.

The two main routes for obtaining images in RGB format are the flatbed scanner and the video camera.

Flatbed scanner

A scanner is a good way of digitizing existing artwork into RGB format. There are many such scanners on the market and both new and existing models are regularly reviewed in the computing press and in industry publications.

Video camera

A video camera mounted as a rostrum camera offers a more versatile path to creating video images than scanners. The main advantage is that there are fewer restrictions on the size and nature of the subject matter. Anything from an illustration in a book to a Wellington boot can be put under the camera and filmed.

It also offers the advantage that you can keep about 250 still images on a video cassette, which can be identified by the time code of the frames they occupy. Each still image will use up about ten seconds of the 2,500 available. The frame-grabber is then programmed to grab a still from the middle of each short sequence of still pictures of the same image using the time-code address.

If you do not have suitable equipment, you may have to use outside facilities, both for obtaining image files in RGB format and for converting the files into any or all of the CD-I image types.

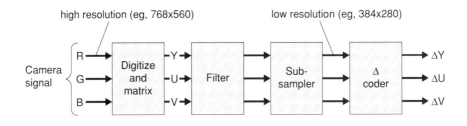

Figure 6.3 The DYUV coding process. ('Δ' – Greek 'delta' – signifies a difference in a quantity.)

Creating and capturing graphic images

Graphic images can be created from scratch on computer graphics systems. There are a variety of graphics and animation programs that create RGB output. The RGB images are encoded using ICUs (Image Conversion Utilities) that run on PCs, Macintoshes or workstations.

The alternative to this approach is to use computer software, such as Adobe's PhotoShop, with special CD-I plug-ins that can convert analogue images directly into the required CD-I format. This type of set-up enables users to fine-tune and validate the CD-I image, and includes paint, colour-correction and dark-room facilities within the same program.

RGB images are converted into the various other formats as follows.

DYUV

If high-resolution DYUV images have to be converted to normal resolution, it is simplest to decode the image first, going back to RGB, and then to encode the image at normal resolution (Figure 6.3).

QHY (Quantized High-Y)

A normal-resolution image is created as for DYUV, and also a high-resolution RGB image. The two images are compared. Chrominance changes are ignored because the eye is not very sensitive to chrominance, but the comparison between the images is used to collect detailed information on luminance changes.

The differences are run-length-encoded. This is a very efficient form of encoding because, when there are very few differences between the two images, it saves having to store lots of zero values. The differences are stored on disc as a separate luminance signal. Typically a QHY signal might use 105 kilobytes of DYUV information, then perhaps 30 kilobytes of difference signal, depending on the differences in the picture.

To play the signal back, the DYUV image is first presented in the normal way; then the difference signal is used to regenerate the extra pixels needed to 'fill in' the picture in order to bring it up to high resolution, restoring it to something very like an RGB image. As a QHY image uses about a quarter as much disc space as a true 768 × 560 image, this technique is extremely useful for an application such as a medical encyclopaedia, in which a very large number of highly detailed images need to be stored on a single disc.

QHY works only on extended-case (not base-case) players and must be used with normal-resolution DYUV on plane A.

Absolute RGB

Images on RGB 555 format use five bits for each of the red, green and blue components. An RGB image uses the space for both picture planes, so the background plane must be switched off.

When coded, a 16-bit word represents one pixel. Red, green and blue each take up five bits, while one bit is the transparency bit.

CLUT encoding

CLUT stands for Colour Look Up Table, a matrix containing the colours that can be used in an image (see page 61). Because each colour in the table can be referred to by its position in the

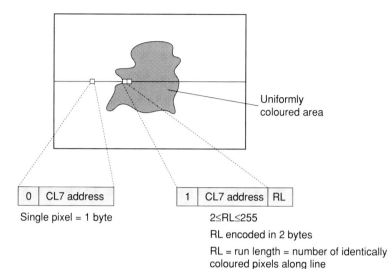

Figure 6.4 Run-length encoding. 'RL' signifies run length. A zero in this position indicates that the run continues to the end of the current line. 'CL7 address' denotes the address of a colour in a CLUT 7 table.

table instead of by specifying its absolute colour value, this is an effective way of saving storage space on the disc.

- CLUT 8 gives 256 colours; it uses the whole look-up table, so it can be used only with plane B set to DYUV or turned off
- CLUT 7 gives 128 colours
- CLUT 4 gives 16 colours; it can be used at high resolution
- CLUT 3 gives eight colours

Run-Length Encoding (RLE)

RLE is suitable for animation and graphics. There are two sorts of RLE image, based upon seven-bit and three-bit CLUT images (Figure 6.4). In seven-bit RLE, single pixels are encoded as single bytes, giving the CLUT code for that pixel. A run of pixels of the same colour is encoded as two bytes, containing the CLUT code and the length of the run (from two to 255 pixels). A length of zero indicates the run extends to the end of the current line of pixels.

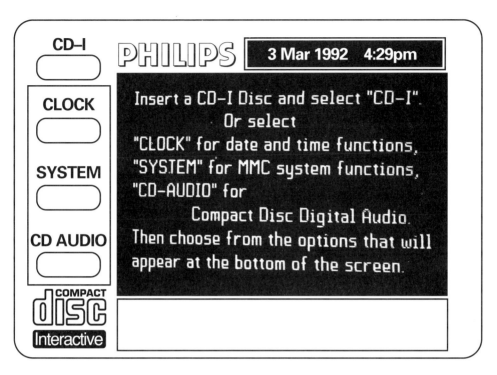

Figure 6.5 A sample of a CD-I player's resident font.

In a three-bit RLE, a pair of three-bit CLUT codes are coded as one byte, and the second byte indicates the length of the run for the pair of pixels. The image types that can be used on each plane are:

Plane A	DYUV, CLUT 8, CLUT 7, CLUT 4, CLUT 7 (RLE), CLUT 3 (RLE)
Plane B	DYUV, CLUT 7, CLUT 4, CLUT 7 (RLE), CLUT 3 (RLE), RGB 555, QHY

Fonts

To display text from ASCII files, the CD-I player must use a set of character-defining codes (the font) in the system. The data for the text comes off the CD-I disc and is combined with the data saying what the text will look like (what typeface, point size, and so on) when the disc is played. The base-case CD-I player contains one resident character set in ROM (Figure 6.5).

This is a useful character set for things like warning messages about system use. If you want something more ornate, many CD-I studios have developed fonts and are now marketing them for the use of CD-I producers. The font details have to be included on the CD-I disc and downloaded when the title is played. You should remember that the bold, italic and roman characters in one point-size each constitute a font.

Animation

Animation is an ideal medium for CD-I. It is expressive and dynamic, and yet it does not use so much space when it is stored digitally as full-motion video 'natural' images. It also suits many of the types of application that are quintessentially CD-I, giving more control on a frame-by-frame basis for such things as education and training, as well as interactive entertainment.

At present the most straightforward path is to develop animation by other means, and then transfer it to CD-I. For a conventional hand-animated film, animation could be converted to CD-I in the same way as any other moving video image – that is, each frame is grabbed by a frame-grabber and digitized, then finally encoded.

Full-motion video coding is cheaper and faster and is suitable for more complex animation graphics. Frame-by-frame RLE, used on the front two planes, is suitable for simpler animations where there are large blocks of colour. This technique saves space on the disc.

Computer animation packages like those available for the PC or the Macintosh can produce files in RGB format that are instantly ready for encoding.

Some features of CD-I and animation

We have noted that animation is especially suited to the CD-I medium. Part of the reason for this is that there is a strong resemblance between the two media. Here are some of their characteristics.

Picture planes and superimposition

A salient feature of animation technique is the separation of foreground and background into planes. The two are often drawn by different artists.This technique means that the background does not have to be redrawn for each frame. Instead, transparent acetate sheets with the foreground action on them are filmed against the same background graphic.

An example of the creative use of CD-I might involve keeping the foreground and background separate and combining them only at runtime (that is, when the title is actually playing). This offers the advantage that different figures can appear against the same background or vice versa, with only a small amount of memory required to store the same reusable bits of information.

Colour

Another feature of hand-animation is the painstaking colouring-in of acetate sheets. While this offers certain advantages in terms of subtle gradations of colour and a pleasant hand-crafted look, it is more difficult to control than the same process on a computer graphics package. Bottles of paint have to be mixed and labelled by hand, whereas a colour that has an RGB digital code is always the same.

CD-I now offers an additional flexibility in image creation. When CD-I graphics are displayed using CLUTs, the image is coloured or painted at runtime. The CLUT is like a palette in which colours are kept at numerical addresses. The data for a CLUT-coded image merely specifies colours at certain addresses in the palette. By changing the colours in the palette, you can change the colours in the image.

This idea has already been exploited to provide a children's animated colouring book. Children can use the CD-I's remote control to choose colours, and a paintbrush-shaped cursor to 'colour in' areas. The animated pictures then appear with the colours they have chosen.

Partial updates and dynamic updates

As mentioned previously, CLUT animation offers a simple way to produce rapid colour alterations such as flashing and twinkling effects. For example, a CLUT 4 producing 16 colours could have alternative colours rapidly loaded in and out, taking up very little memory and producing the effect of far more colours than are actually being used at any one instant. Dynamic updates (re-freshing the CLUT palette as each line of the screen is painted) extend the possibilities of CLUT animation even further.

Audio

Audio encoding

When a sound is recorded digitally, it is not recorded continu-ously (as with analogue methods) but sampled at intervals.

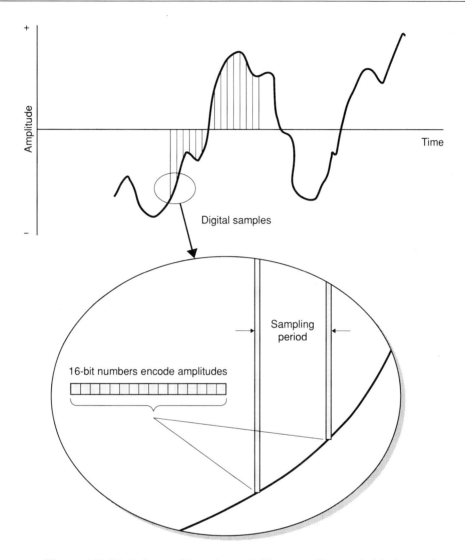

Figure 6.6 Digital recording of sound. The sampling period is inversely proportional to the rate of sampling; for example, 22.7 microseconds corresponds to a rate of 44.1 kHz.

Samples are like the dots that make up a photograph in a newspaper: the more dots, the smoother the picture looks. The number of samples taken in a fixed period of time is known as the sampling frequency.

The amount of data recorded about each sample is known as the amplitude. The greater the amplitude, the more detail is recorded, and the more accurately the sound is reproduced. For example, 32 bits can record more about a sound than 16 bits can. The quality of sound recording that results also depends upon the sampling frequency. However, sounds recorded with a higher sampling frequency and amplitude take up more data space. Figure 6.6 shows how digitally recorded sound is encoded.

Two methods of encoding sound are used by CD-I. They are PCM (Pulse-Code Modulation) and ADPCM (Adaptive Delta Pulse-Code Modulation).

Pulse-Code Modulation (PCM)

This is the method of digitizing analogue sound waves by sampling them at fixed intervals. It records a value for each sample, and so is comparatively expensive in terms of data storage. It is the technique used for ordinary audio compact discs, and results in a very high quality of sound reproduction. In CD-I, PCM is used to record at a frequency of 44.1 kHz (1 kHz = 1000 hertz, or cycles per second), with 16-bit amplitude for each stereo channel. Each sample requires 32 bits (16 bits per channel).

Adaptive Delta Pulse-Code Modulation (ADPCM)

ADPCM is like pulse-code modulation except that in the process of digitizing the sound the differences between successive samples, rather than their absolute values, are recorded.

There are four levels of sound quality: CD-DA, Level A, Level B and Level C. Each format is suitable for different purposes and is available in mono or stereo. The quality of sound is determined by the sampling frequency and the number of data bits used per sample. Table 6.1 shows how sampling frequency and bits per sample relate to audio quality.

Table 6.1 CD-I sound-quality levels.

Level (requirement)	Sampling rate	Bandwidth	Number of channels	Fraction of CD-I data rate used per channel
CD digital audio (super hi-fi)	44.1 kHz	20 kHz	1 stereo	1/1
CD-I ADCPM				
A (Hi-fi music mode – equivalent to LP)	37.8 kHz	17 kHz	2 stereo 4 mono	1/2 1/4
B (Hi-fi music mode – equivalent to FM broadcast)	37.8 kHz	17 kHz	4 stereo 8 mono	1/4 1/8
C (quality speech mode – equivalent to AM broadcast)	18.9 kHz	8.5 kHz	8 stereo 16 mono	1/8 1/16

Recording audio for CD-I

Digital recording is now a well established art. DAT (Digital Audio Tape) recorders can be used, and sophisticated computer software can control the recording process. For example, software (such as Digidesign DECK) that emulates a multitrack digital audio recording deck can be used. This allows unlimited digital track bouncing, overdubbing, MIDI file playback and automated mixing.

Converting audio into PCM digital format

When sound has been recorded in either format – analogue (any format) or digital (DAT) – a number of devices exist for use on PCs or Macintoshes to convert them into PCM files held on a hard disc or other storage device. All audio must initially be converted into PCM form.

These devices are currently available as slot-in cards for personal computers. They record at 44.1 or 48 kHz and have a signal-to-noise ratio (SNR) of about 85–90 dB, providing 16- or 32-bit sound.

Manipulating and editing audio

Audio is manipulated and edited in PCM format on a computer, which can be an Apple Macintosh, an IBM-compatible or a workstation.

Both the PC and the Macintosh have friendly interfaces for completing this job. The terminal displays the sound waves on the screen at the same time as it plays the relevant snatch of music. Users can 'swipe' a given segment, mark it and carry out a number of operations – invert, reverse, replace or smooth. They can also enhance or modify the signal – compress or expand it, convert the sample rate, shift the pitch and introduce non-destructive fade-in or fade-out effects. Microsounds from Microtechnology is one of the packages available in this area.

Converting PCM to ADPCM

The final stage in producing files ready to be slotted into place on the CD-I is to convert the audio from PCM to ADPCM. Conversion to ADPCM is done using ACUs (Audio Conversion Utilities), which run on PCs, Macintoshes or workstations (Figure 6.7).

Once the files have been created, the production team can listen to them and carry out some further editing (such as cutting pieces of music to the right length). Remember to keep a copy of the PCM original in case the section you have converted turns out to be inappropriate, or at the wrong quality level, or of the wrong length.

Figure 6.7 Audio editing using a Macintosh computer.

What do you need?
Recording equipment – either analogue or digital DAT
PCM conversion equipment
ADPCM conversion equipment
Materials in analogue or digital format

Conclusion

Gathering, editing and processing materials are major components of CD-I production. The requirements of each project will differ, but all types of information for inclusion on the disc will need to be processed in some way to become suitable for CD-I. Using digital recording techniques wherever possible, for sound, still images and full-motion video, will save time and reduce the number of steps required to turn each item into the appropriate CD-I format.

The producer's and management team's roles at this stage of the process will probably be to ensure that the right facilities are available, and that sounds and images are converted into the appropriate formats by the technical staff responsible for this stage of production.

If complex computer software is to be used, it is a good idea to make sure that the staff using it are sufficiently familiar with it to complete their tasks efficiently before work begins. Software is frequently updated and someone should take responsibility for keeping an eye on developments that may be useful for CD-I, such as new file filters.

7

Authoring

Introduction

Authoring is the process of turning all the source material – whether it has been gathered, recorded or converted – into a finished, structured programme, ready to be put down on disc for production and sale. Some production staff will be involved only with this direct creation of a CD-I programme, but this can include a wide range of tasks, to cover all of these functions:

- sequencing material and scripting
- writing text files
- adding multimedia features, such as menus and hotspots, that respond to user input
- managing memory and technical functions
- getting the best out of finite resources, such as the player's data stream or bandwidth

Within the authoring process there are several discrete stages, which most CD-I projects will pass through. These can be summarized as:

(1) prototyping
(2) authoring/programming
(3) disc-building
(4) emulation
(5) testing and validation

In this and the following chapters we will be looking at these five processes and at the way they interact in the production of a CD-I. Then we shall move on to look at ways of managing them and ensuring that a large CD-I project can move through them smoothly, however many staff members, skills and processes are involved.

It is important in managing the production process for the whole programme to make realistic schedules and start dates for the authoring process. In some projects, the programmers may need far more time than the designers, so that you have to start software development long before all the audio-visual materials are ready. But in others the pre-development of ready-to-use software engines may mean that there is very little programming to be done, and the authoring stage is very brief. Software engines are discussed in more detail later in this chapter.

Prototyping

This is the process of building a working model of your intended programme. How elaborate or sketchy the prototype is, and the amount of effort expended on its production, will depend on a number of factors:

- the size and complexity of the programme
- the time, resources and skills available
- the extent to which the prototype is reusable
- the sophistication of the prototyping tool being used

The stage at which prototyping begins will vary from project to project. For some programmes, the designers may have found it appropriate to develop a small-scale prototype of a programme segment very early on, in order to have something to demonstrate to secure funding, or to see whether a planned effect critical to the programme design would really work in practice.

Whenever the prototype is begun, it is good practice to have a working model of at least part of the programme before full-scale production of the planned programme begins. This enables potential problems in the design to be ironed out before too much effort has been wasted and shows new staff, recruited to the team for the production stages, what the results of their labours should look like.

Making a prototype

There is nothing to stop a programmer producing the prototype from scratch, using a high-level computer language such as C. But this is an impractical approach in most situations, because there are a number of specialized CD-I prototyping tools available, as well as simple generic multimedia authoring programs. These allow anything from a reasonable facsimile of the final programme to a set of hypermedia notes, demonstrating programme structure, to be produced quickly and easily.

Many of these programs are straightforward to use, so that the designer or producer can create the prototype, without any need to involve specialist programmers. Some of them are already in use among designers, so that they do not need to be learned; these include HyperCard, SuperCard, and Philips' CD-I MediaMogul.

These will produce something that has the 'look and feel' of the final programme. The design team can use the prototyping tool to experiment and to give the client or other commissioning party some idea of what the final programme will be like. For this reason, approval of the prototype is often one of the project milestones, after which the programming team can start work. Perhaps more commonly, the prototyping becomes an iterative process, in which the prototype is reviewed, amended, tested, reviewed and so on, until it is good enough.

It is important to remember that this *is* a prototype. Spending too much time and energy on it can eat into budgets that would be better spent on the actual programme. It is not meant to be absolutely perfect, although it should save time and money on the actual production by resolving problems and helping the team organize full-scale production better. The prototype is simply meant to demonstrate whether or not the proposed ideas and ways of doing things will work.

From prototyping to authoring

In the early days of CD-I, there was a clear distinction between prototyping and fully fledged authoring. This distinction still exists to some extent, but is becoming blurred, largely because of the development of new authoring packages and script-to-disc conversion routines. Packages purely for prototyping are quick and easy to use and useful for producing demonstrations and models. However, they do not usually produce a real-time interleaved file. So for producing a real programme, to professional standards, the production team has to turn to a professional authoring system or programming language.

Because of this, some designers and producers prefer to do the whole CD-I job, from prototyping to final testing and validation, using a single package. Others mix and match packages, using different hardware and software for different parts of the production process; perhaps prototyping on an Apple Macintosh, then transferring the work to a package such as MediaMogul for authoring.

The prototyping tool will probably allow you to produce scripts, or some kind of controlling logic for the disc. The script translates the logic and structure of the CD-I design into an actual programme. It is not the same as the text of the programme, which is a script in the traditional sense of the word. This CD-I script can be produced by using an authoring package, or by programming from scratch, or by using program sections that have already been written. It is used to:

- implement effects, such as cuts
- supervise interactivity
- synchronize audio and video sequences
- load new audio or video images
- control the player's memory
- keep track of the CD-I's status

- structure the materials on the disc
- control the input and output of information
- manage the technical functions of the player

You can exercise varying degrees of control over these functions. With a prototype you are less concerned with a polished result and can leave your software to take care of any low-level technical work that needs to be done. You can concentrate on implementing an interactive structure, choosing effects, building up a script for the programme. To produce a finished programme you may want more control over the results, the effects used and so on. A more sophisticated authoring tool or a custom-written program will be more appropriate here.

Your team of programmers, using high-level computer languages such as C to create effects from scratch, will provide much more power and flexibility in turning the programme design into reality. They have more freedom to define the way the audio-visual information is accessed and presented. They are controlling the information more directly and can address the player at a more technical level. Because of this, programmers can achieve effects that are not possible when prototyping. The prototyping system keeps things simple, but in doing so has to make compromises and so offers a more limited set of options to the author. A programming language is not simple, but the range of options it offers is virtually unlimited.

The line between prototyping and full authoring is becoming blurred because of the increasing sophistication of prototyping systems. These now allow authors to use programming techniques, such as subroutines and variables, within scripts that are written in English rather than computer code. The experienced user of a prototyping system can use it as a high-level programming tool, while a newcomer may stick to producing straightforward scripts.

Bear in mind that the more customization and programming facilities a package has, the more programming skills it takes to use. A logical, modular approach may be as essential in using a prototyping tool as in programming. Such an approach is likely to include structured script designs, the ability to fix bugs systematically and a methodical approach to documentation.

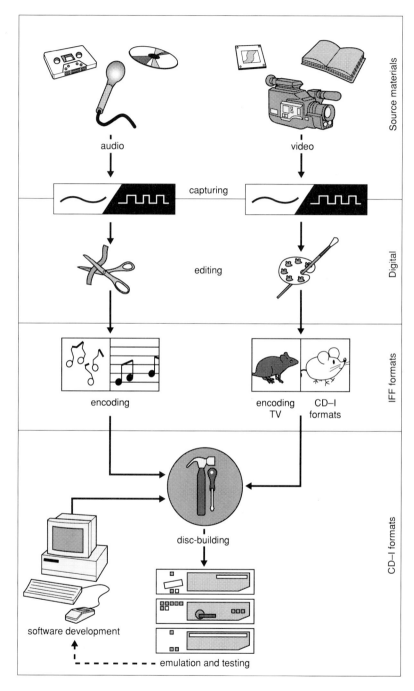

Figure 7.1 The authoring process.

Authoring

Authoring packages manage the CD-I production process and make it much easier to come up with the finished programme. Sophisticated authoring environments will enable you to turn the materials you have gathered in digital formats into a finished programme, ready to be pressed and delivered to the client. They include many features to ease and automate as much of the process as possible. The current generation of packages goes well beyond simply imposing an interactive structure on materials. CD-I authoring can include the processes listed below (see also Figure 7.1):

- prototyping (iterative process)
- programming/authoring
- script-to-disc conversion
- disc-building
- amendment (iterative process)
- emulation
- optimizing/pre-mastering
- writing master tape

Software engines to automate production

Remember that not all programmes will need programming or even detailed authoring work. This is especially true where a series of discs is being produced, or where software engines are in use. A software engine is a routine that carries out a standard set of functions and that has been pre-written by a programmer or author. Each programme in the series can make use of the software engine, to save logic and scripts being rewritten for each new programme. It is quite possible to automate the authoring of an entire CD-I programme in this way, although in most cases software engines will deal with subsections of programmes rather than the entire thing.

For instance, the logic to handle up to five interactive hotspots and branch off to five destinations may be ready-written as a software engine. The author/programmer simply calls the relevant routine whenever such a screen is needed. Of course, the development of the software engines themselves takes time, and will require the programmers to analyse the design and see which parts of the programme have a similar structure, so that their production can be automated. Although such sections would use the same software engine repeatedly, they would actually look quite different because the engine would be calling up different images and graphics.

In a series of, say, six CD-Is, the first programme would require input to prepare the software engines and to design some tools for the designers to use on the later programmes. The later programmes could then be put together simply by coding the relevant data and using a high-level authoring package that could use the engines and tools developed for the series. In this way, software engines automate aspects of the CD-I production process.

Of course, it is often the case that one particular requirement overrides the others. For instance, you may want the copyright protection on your disc to be as tough as possible, and you may therefore adopt a programming approach because it allows you to build in a better security system.

Authoring versus programming

The authoring and programming routes to CD-I development each have their advantages and weaknesses. Let's take an example that applies to many CD-I programmes, animation.

There is a choice between using an authoring system, such as CD-I Author running on a workstation, and a prototyping system, such as MediaMogul on a dedicated CD-I system. What effect will the choice have on the eventual product?

Prototyping tools give easy access to CLUT animation through their built-in Paint programs. It would be fast and simple to develop an animated sequence. However, it would not be able to include complex effects. For example, you might want a graphic to move around the screen in response to the user moving a joystick. CLUT animation would not be able to cope with this, because too many options for the next sprite position would need to be loaded simultaneously.

For this reason, although other aspects of the programme could be tested satisfactorily using a prototyping tool, you might decide to test this function by writing a small piece of code and perhaps calling it as a subroutine in the prototyping tool. Using programming tools and techniques, such as those available with CD-I Author, an array of the sprites would be held in memory. The programmer would drive the animation by ensuring that the right frame, containing the sprite in the relevant position, would be displayed when the user moved the joystick. The animation would take longer to develop, but would be more flexible and might allow a higher-quality graphic to be used.

For fast-moving and highly visual CD-I programmes, such as action games, which need to exploit the video capabilities of the system to its absolute limits, it will almost always be preferable to employ specialist programmers with computer games experience. For less demanding programmes, the right authoring environment will provide access to all the CD-I features needed and will deal with many technical complexities automatically.

Choosing an authoring system

One of the benefits of CD-I is that the producer is not restricted to proprietary systems but can choose from a range of hardware and software. Machines and packages can be mixed and linked if necessary, until the producer has a prototyping/authoring facility that exactly matches the requirements of the project and the expertise, budget and staff available. Some of the criteria to consider are listed in the box.

Complex programme

special effects	*complex interactivity*
complex logical structures	*demanding applications*
full-motion video	*long programme*
use of software engines	*high level of security needed*
programming staff available	

Straightforward programme

straightforward video/audio	*simple interactivity*
basic logical structure	*short programme*
no need for software engines, or	*staff not specialist programmers*
software engines already in place	*prototype or trial programme*

Get help from outside

There are several ways of deciding which mix of hardware and software will be best. An increasingly popular method is to brief an independent multimedia consultant, who will weigh up the resources you currently have, your budget, the demands of the programme and so on. He or she will then make recommendations and possibly provide costings for hardware and software. You may wish to ask for a brief report, listing the options that were rejected, with the reasons. On the other hand, you may want to deal more informally with the consultant, perhaps through a meeting or advice session at which you jointly discuss the various possibilities.

The time of such consultants is not cheap, but they can often save their clients a great deal more money than they charge them. They do this in two ways: by explaining the most cost-effective way of achieving the required result, and by preventing the purchase of an unsuitable machine and software.

Work out your requirements

Some CD-I producers, who perhaps already have some experience of choosing and using computer graphics and multimedia systems, may prefer to select their own systems.

One way of choosing the authoring system is to draw up a 'wish list'. This is a list of all the features you would ideally like the equipment to have. You end up with the specification of the perfect system for your production team and programme plans. You then take this perfect profile and use it to assess the hardware and software currently available. Using the profile helps you to see which mix of equipment comes closest to your perfect set-up. The process of drawing up the list also helps you to distinguish between what you really must have and what it would merely be nice to have; and to work out what equipment needs to be bought, or leased to be available to your team all the time, and what will be needed for only part of the project and is best hired when needed from a facilities house.

Build on what you have already

One of the great benefits of multimedia is its flexibility. It is possible to get a long way down the production path of a CD-I programme while still using tried and trusted production methods familiar from previous, non CD-I projects. Many aspects of the programme can be produced using standard computer and audio-visual equipment; many graphics and multimedia authoring packages can export files in CD-I formats.

It may well be far more efficient to develop materials and scripts on a system you're already familiar with, transferring to a CD-I environment quite far on in the production process. The availability of CD-I emulators is a key part of this flexibility and is discussed in more detail from page 134 onwards.

Training

Most producers of authoring packages offer training to users and potential users. In addition, Philips' own studios offer general courses on various aspects of CD-I design and production, which introduce a range of authoring tools. Well-run courses offer designers and producers a good way to sample different CD-I tools, learn new skills and discover more about the way authoring programs work than they might learn in unstructured experimentation with products. One CD-I designer reports: 'These programs can be very complex, even though they're intended to be easy to use. We benefited a lot from the training courses we attended.'

Conclusion

Deciding the route by which the CD-I design will become a finished programme is one of the main responsibilities of the producer. It will have an impact on the number and type of staff recruited for the project, the kind of equipment and facilities bought or hired for the project and the way the finished programme appears.

Simple authoring systems of some kind should be made available to the design team to enable a prototype to be developed. One or many prototypes or sample programme segments may need to be produced and ideally this should be done as cheaply as possible.

However, for production of the programme itself, a more sophisticated authoring system may be needed, or the complexity of the planned programme may require complete custom programming. Using an authoring package will enable some economies to be made; software engines can be written that can be used throughout a programme or series of programmes.

8

Using authoring software

Introduction

Authoring packages allow producers to build multimedia programmes without getting involved in low-level computer programming. The different packages on the market vary greatly
in the way they approach this. Some make authoring an extremely simple process, a matter of selecting a few options from
a menu, but in doing so restrict the options available. Others
offer a great deal of freedom to authors, effectively allowing
custom computer programs to be created without programming,
but make much greater demands on the users' skills. In this
section we have used a general example, as typical as possible,
of an authoring package – but there are an increasing number
available, with a wide variety of approaches.

   Authoring packages tend to divide the process into three
main activities, each of which typically has its own separate
editor:

- image editor

- sequence or script editor

- menu editor

In a sense these editors work at three different levels (Figure
8.1). The image editor, working at the foundation level, allows
you to create or edit text, graphics and other visual materials
that are stored on a hard disc. Then, using the sequence editor,

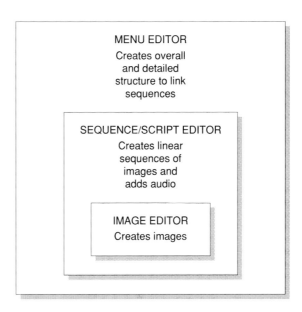

Figure 8.1 The relationships among editors.

you can build these materials into scripts, which may combine video and audio and have specific instructions on timing, effects and so on. The menu editor is for creating the superstructure – the interactive control that will run the finished scripts, allow branching from hotspots and so on. (See Figure 8.2.)

The rest of this chapter looks in more detail at the three editors, and at ways of getting the best out of whichever authoring packages are used in your studios.

The image editor

Once all the visual assets for use in the intended programme have been assembled, they will probably need to be processed in some way. Images may need to be scaled or cropped, or to have captions added. This is where the image editor begins to

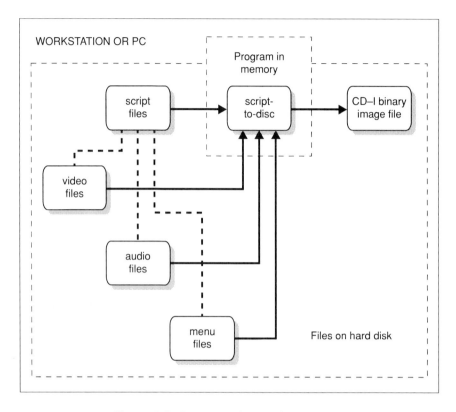

Figure 8.2 Creating a binary CD-I image.

be useful (Figure 8.3). One of its main uses is to pull in video that has previously been digitized, so that it can be worked on further. The image editor (or similar facility) will usually allow you to:

- draw, paint, fill, shade and so on
- scale and transform images
- manipulate CLUT images
- merge two pictures into one CLUT
- use mosaic and smudge (edge-softening) functions

As well as the usual software drawing and painting capabilities, the image editor offers several different text fonts. These can be used for superimposing captions and headings on the video stills.

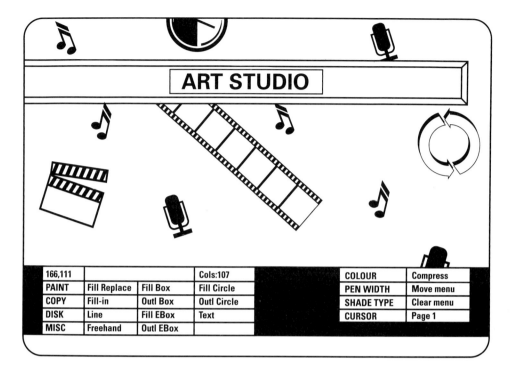

ART STUDIO

166,111			Cols:107		COLOUR	Compress
PAINT	Fill Replace	Fill Box	Fill Circle		PEN WIDTH	Move menu
COPY	Fill-in	Outl Box	Outl Circle		SHADE TYPE	Clear menu
DISK	Line	Fill EBox	Text		CURSOR	Page 1
MISC	Freehand	Outl EBox				

Figure 8.3 MediaMogul's Art Studio graphics utility screen.

Extra animation effects are available with some authoring systems. For instance, animation sequences created in a different graphical environment can be integrated into the CD-I programme (often as video transition effects).

Templates

As part of its prototyping facilities, the image editor will probably include a number of ready-made tools and templates for you to use if you wish to save time. Some systems are also supplied with the CD-I equivalent of clip art: a selection of on-screen buttons, arrows, borders and so on will have been prepared, so that you can use and modify them in your own programme's interface.

The audio-visual materials do not all have to be ready before authoring begins. The author can use 'placeholder' graphics and audio files while testing the script. These are files, of a type similar to the intended ones, that can be used as dummies. When the actual materials are ready, they can be substituted at the appropriate points in the script. For example, if an animation is not ready but the soundtrack needs to be worked on, a clip-art animation could be used as a placeholder. The soundtrack can be married to the finished visuals later.

The sequence/script editor

Sequencing and scripting begin the process of turning assets into a recognizable CD-I programme. The script builds parts of the programme as the viewer will see it after selecting a programme segment from a menu. It is at this point that video effects are added to the converted materials; it is the first time that each video item will have been sequenced with the items that are likely to precede or follow it. Ensuring that the transition between items is smooth and well managed is important for good-quality CD-I programmes.

Mature CD-I authoring environments endeavour to make scripting as simple as possible without reducing the options available to the producer. One way in which this is done is to allow the programme author to control sound and video assets as icons, or as entries in an easily comprehensible table. Assets are simply added to the table, either as icons or by file name, at the appropriate time point. Events such as video transition effects and the playing of sound samples and soundmaps are also specified in terms of the precise time at which the author wants them to happen.

Typical CD-I sequence editors are graphical tools and have a screen layout similar to that shown in Figure 8.4. You can scroll horizontally through the programme, as far your script has progressed. The author builds scripts by specifying any or all of these items in one column:

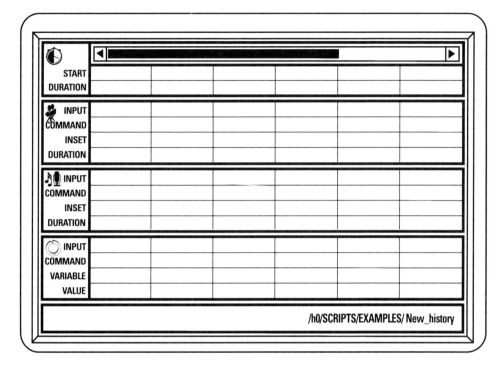

Figure 8.4 The MediaMogul script-editor screen.

- timing of events
- a video file
- an audio file
- any effects for audio/video timing transitions
- control information, especially menu files produced by the menu editor

In the case of the audio and video files, the author tells the authoring system where to find the file on the hard disk. Effects will include all the popular video effects: dissolve, wipe, curtain close/open, and fade; and similarly for audio: play, loop, pause and fade.

A helpful feature of many sequence editors is a graphical interface, which allows users to select an image or sound sequence by clicking in the column or box and selecting the required file from a pop-up menu. It is also easy to rearrange and reorganize items and, with most authoring environments, to play back work in progress to see how it is shaping up. Once a sequence has been created the author runs it, notes any changes he or she wishes to make, then goes back to the scripting screen and edits the sequence. Each sequence is saved as a file with its own name, so that it can easily be identified, by both the menu editor and the human producer, for linking into the overall programme structure and for any further editing work that is required.

Changes can often be made very simply – for example, by selecting a different effect as the transition between two images, or by adding a different soundtrack to a section. A programme segment can look radically different after just a few mouse clicks. While this can allow for exciting experimentation, there is the drawback that the ease of changing programmes can encourage unnecessary fiddling and fine-tuning. If the original programme design specifies a particular transition between a set of images, it may not be necessary or practical to try out every option your authoring package allows at the production stage to see what they look like.

A much better approach is to ensure that the designers and production staff have had plenty of opportunity to use and experiment with the authoring software, so that the programme design exploits it to the best and no-one is left with the feeling that it should have been done differently.

Script samples

Most authoring systems include sample scripts as part of the package. A good way of learning how the software works is to look at a sample script, run it, see how it works in practice and then study the script again. If you don't have your own CD-I programme materials ready, using the samples can be a good way to become familiar with the effects available and to provide basic editing practice.

Most tools will include sample mini CD-I programmes that you can learn from. Modifying these ready-scripted programmes and gauging the results can be a very effective way of getting to grips with the way the authoring software works.

The menu editor

The final part of the CD-I programme design to be implemented is the overall interactive structure of the programme. This is put into place with the authoring package's menu editor.

The flowcharts or storyboards drawn up during the detailed design stage define the structure of the planned programme. The flowchart may exist on paper, or as a simple prototype in a hypermedia program, or even as a roughly produced file generated by the authoring package itself. The menu editor allows authors to implement this planned structure by adding interactive hotspots to pictures or graphics, and associating these with script files produced using the sequence/script editor (see Figure 8.5). Now, when a button is pressed on screen, it really will take the viewer to the chosen segment of the programme, which already exists as a scripted programme sequence.

Creating hotspots

Using the menu editor, the author can load a video image, then outline the area that is to form the hotspot. The author then specifies which sequences are to be played and displayed when the user selects that hotspot. When the hotspot is activated by the viewer, the associated script is called and played.

This script is known as the destination script, and the movement from menu to programme segment is called 'branching'. The term 'branching' means following a logical path from one part of the programme to another, often as a result of selecting a menu item. The internal logical structure of a programme is seen as a tree-shaped diagram, with each menu a place where several branches split off from a larger branch or the trunk.

The style and on-screen appearance of menus and hotspots will have been specified during the design phase; what is being implemented now is the structure in the programme script that will ensure that when the viewer selects a menu item by

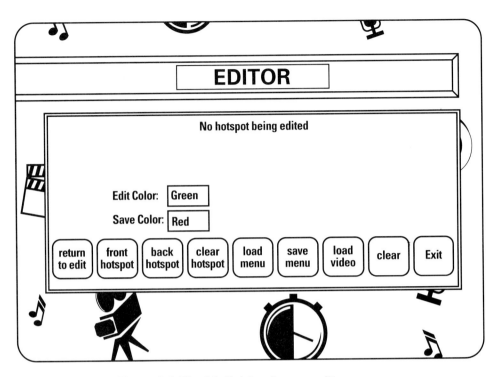

Figure 8.5 The MediaMogul menu-editor screen.

clicking on a hotspot, the desired action results and the programme moves on to the chosen place.

Playing back the programme

During the prototyping phase, the designer/producer may want
to get a rough idea of what the real thing, the finished programme,
will look like. To do this, there is no need to build a real-time file
and play it on a real CD-I player. Most software that will allow
you to prototype will also allow you to play the file you have
created on the hard disk of your development system. Obviously this is only an approximation to the way it will look when

it is played in real time. The system will not interleave the files, but will simply fetch and carry files containing images and sounds.

Nevertheless, this can be a useful first stage in seeing whether it is worth developing an idea further and in learning how to use the authoring system. A discussion of how real-time files are produced from authoring systems begins on page 130.

Conclusion

Simple authoring systems can provide an easy route into CD-I production, especially for companies and individuals with small budgets who need to put more effort into producing and editing source material than into programming complex CD-I effects. The output of the script and menu editors can be converted by 'script-to-disc' software into a form that will, together with the audio and video files, allow a CD-I disc to be made directly.

The authoring software will also help in the organization and management of the production process by demanding particular inputs at particular stages. The provision of prototyping and playback facilities encourages one to test ideas and revise and iterate the programme as work progresses – all good working practices.

However, even the simplest authoring software is powerful and takes time to learn. Using the samples, the clip art and the programme scripts supplied is a good way to become familiar with any package, but in the end nothing can really supplant experience gained from real-world use of a program.

9

Programming

Introduction

Programming is a critical part of CD-I production and perhaps the most technically demanding. Although it is possible, using some authoring systems, to produce a CD-I title without any custom programming, this will be appropriate only for small, low-budget projects where a simple programme with few visual and other effects is needed.

However, there is some overlap between using an authoring system and programming. Some authoring systems include programming features, such as the use of variables and the ability to call subroutines, and may require someone with programming expertise to operate them. And some programming environments go under the name of authoring systems. This is not really surprising, given the flexibility of the CD-I environment.

The absence of rigid demarcations between one production method and another is one of CD-I's great strengths. Accordingly, this chapter refers to 'programmers'. But bear in mind that these people could be using high-level computer languages such as C, the CD-I operating system CD-RTOS, assembly languages, sophisticated authoring systems or a combination of these.

What is as important as the tools programmers use is the approach they take, and non-programmers using authoring systems can learn much from programming methodology.

Although producing a CD-I programme may seem worlds away from developing a database or financial system, programmers apply the same meticulous way of working in order to get the results they want.

The specification

Before the programmers can start their work, they will need to produce, or to be given, their own specification of the work to be done. They will use the detailed document produced at the end of the design phase as the basis for a technical specification, based on an analysis of the programming input that the design seems to require. This is a very traditional programming approach, with a technical and functional specification mapping out the work to be done and a testing and validation specification to check everything. But programming for multimedia is 'inherently complicated' and the traditional methodical approach is as valid here as in any other type of programming.

The technical specification has several functions. It identifies the design approach that the software team is going to take, which needs to be consistent from programmer to programmer. It should be sufficiently detailed for different development areas to be identified and assigned to different members of the team, so that, say, one programmer can work on video effects and another on a software engine to automate production of all the menus in a programme segment.

The specification should include a global set of standards or rules for the project. Although people will be working separately on different sections, the sections must fit together, so some ground rules are essential.

The natural breakdown of programming tasks will often be suggested by the structure of the title. A Philips CD-I programmer says:

'On a big project our approach is to break the programme design into major subsystems, from the point of view that some sections will be bespoke programs for the project, such as the game in the

Golf Museum disc, and other sections will become generic, reusable software engines – for example, the code that plays audio-visual.'

Validating the design

Once the title has been broken down into its components, the software team looks at the way the audio-visual effects are going to be achieved. A programmer describes the process in this way:

'For each section we think about how we're going to implement it, in terms of the hardware. This is where we start thinking "We'll use two planes here, and one plane there, and we'll use RLE to do the animation." This is where we start thinking about the player hardware, too. Is it feasible to do it? And if it is, what is the rough set-up of the machine at each stage? And here we start thinking about memory as well: roughly how much memory is going to be taken up?'

The designers, of course, have a pretty clear idea of what the player can do and will have kept this in mind while producing their design. However, many programmers feel that designers should not be curbed by what they feel to be the machine's limitations. Programmers can often find new ways of achieving effects that at first seemed impossible. However, this requires trust between programmers and producer that what is being offered can be achieved by the time it will be needed for the programme. Sometimes it may be better to play safe and persuade the programmers to stay within the limits of what can be guaranteed to work.

No matter how much a system can deliver, expert programmers will always try to get the system to do more. Here's a programmer talking about the kind of technical challenge found at the very ambitious end of CD-I production:

'We had 180 a-v shows, each lasting about a minute and a half. If you do a quick calculation, you find that if you use the standard technique of real-time files, where you put pictures and audio together, it just wouldn't fit on a disc, and the timing problems would be horrendous. So we designed the a-v Presenter, which discards all the empty sectors, and now we can fit everything onto a disc. To do that we had to evolve the a-v engine, and it runs off instructions like "show a picture" or "play audio", all that sort of thing, so we needed to write an assembler and a special disc-builder to do that.'

The programming environment

A general point to note is that, at the time of writing, a large amount of hard-disk storage is necessary. An optical disc can contain 600 MB of data. The programmer's hard disk will therefore need to be about 750 MB, unformatted, simply to contain the audio-visual materials, program code and so on. An equal amount of space will then be necessary to store and run the compiled disc image.

One disk is used to store the data and audio-visual sources. The other is used to store the master copy of the title. However, this area is changing fast and there are signs that a system that uses a single source file may be available in the near future.

Philips' CD-I Author is an example of a complete programming environment, which consists of four basic elements:

- IMS Programmer's Toolkit
- Balboa Runtime Environment
- master disc-building program
- emulation program

This section looks at the first two of these elements in more detail. The other two are discussed in the following chapter.

The IMS Programmer's Toolkit

Toolkits, such as the IMS Programmer's Toolkit, are essential for speeding up the programmer's job. They usually contain a number of utilities. Image-conversion utilities convert PC or Macintosh graphics to an appropriate CD-I format; similarly, there are audio-conversion utilities. For more information on conversion, see Chapter 6.

The toolkit will probably also contain OS-9 cross-compiler and assembler libraries. One of the requirements of working on a variety of hardware platforms is to recompile libraries when the platform is changed. A cross-compiler will operate with both MS-DOS and Macintosh operating systems, allowing the programmer access to a variety of libraries while still maintaining compatibility with the existing OS-9 compiler. For instance, CD-I disc-building and conversion of video to IFF format can both be carried out in MPW, the Macintosh programming environment.

The Balboa Runtime Environment

When programmers worked on early CD-I titles, they had to write routines from scratch. They often had to start from first principles, using the technical specification of CD-I (the Green Book) as their starting-point.

The routines those programmers developed have now been collected into a library of CD-I programming utilities, so that other programmers can take advantage of the work that has already been done. For instance, there is ready-written display management software. This manages the interface between the CD-RTOS kernel and the display.

One example is Philips' Balboa Runtime Environment (Figure 9.1). Balboa removes the need for the programmer to get to grips with the detailed technical working of the CD-I hardware. It also provides hierarchical action facilities that help the programmer to design code that will work well in an interactive environment. This is often called 'virtual' programming.

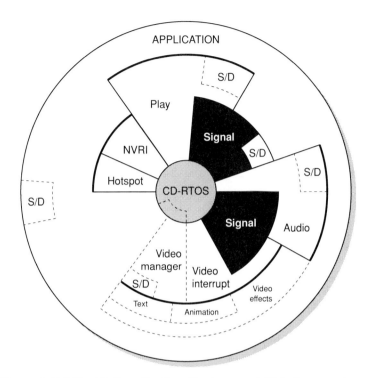

Figure 9.1 Philips' Balboa Runtime Environment. This diagram shows the organization of the hierarchy of managers that lie between the real-time operating system, CD-RTOS, and the application. 'S/D' denotes 'Status and debug manager'.

The whole concept of Balboa is flexibility. You can always add your own functions to the library. You may want to do this where you have an application that is optimized for a particular function. Or again, you may wish to buy selected functions developed by some of the software companies now working in this area. A programmer can also write directly for CD-RTOS and add in Balboa functions, so it offers a flexible way of programming.

The Balboa library includes:

- an engine for dispatching functions when they are called
- an engine for processing signals
- a modular architecture of 16 managers, which allows more than one logical program to run at any given time

Balboa managers	
Video display	Video resources
Video interrupt callbacks	Video effects (wipes, dissolves and so on)
Audio delivery and play	Font text output
Animation display	
OS-9 signal handling	Timer intervals
Buffer delivery of assets	Non-volatile RAM handling
Status reporting	
Cursor display and management	Hotspot setup and management
User input recording	User interaction control

Software engines

Software engines were discussed briefly in the last chapter. Here we look at their use from the programmer's point of view.

A software engine is a piece of code that can be used repeatedly in one or more titles. The use and development of software engines are closely related to the issue of modular design.

For instance, as programmers develop certain tools, they can add a user interface that allows the graphics designer to use the tool. In this way, some production functions can be moved from the programming to the design domain. In fact, if a series of titles is planned, this technique can cut costs enormously on the follow-up titles.

Experienced developers feel that CD-I lends itself to an object-oriented, modular approach. One element of the plan has total responsibility for everything: the screen and all other active components. When it has finished it cleans up after itself and passes control to the next phase. So, for instance, where a menu branches down to another section, the menu would be a separate module or engine and the application that is called from the menu would again be a separate module. The two would reside independently in memory. A CD-I programmer comments:

> 'We look to see if we can produce some generic software that we could use for future projects. If we identify some reusable software, we tend to give it the name "manager" and that piece of software could possibly appear in other titles in future. So you tend to find modules and managers being talked about in the specifications.'

In fact, some producers also talk about an 'engine-oriented production cycle'. There are cases where so much of the software consists of reusable engines that entire programmes can be turned around in six weeks or less. In other instances, more effort may be spent on programming some sections, to make the code suitable for reuse in future projects and save time overall in a series of discs. In practice most CD-I studios will have their own standard code for dealing with many standard situations, and only a small amount of custom programming will need to be done for individual projects.

Managing memory

Even with one megabyte of memory in the player, strategies for effective allocation and deallocation of memory are important. A major factor in programme design is the quantity of data in the player's memory at a given point and how fast the response time will be. So the software team will draw up a specification of:

- how much memory the title will need
- how much space real-time files, for instance, will take up
- how much graphic data there is (this is often worked out by getting sample graphics screens and testing them to see how much space they take up)

If algorithms need to be written, they will probably be written and tested at this stage. Real-time files, for instance, are loaded and run instantaneously and this is ideal for some techniques. But sometimes you may want a bigger screen area, and this is easier to achieve if you buffer data in memory.

If a CD-I title features, for example, an interactive game, then memory management will be especially important, and this will be reflected in the specification. The software designers may construct a table to show the major techniques to be used in the game and the major pieces of data that are involved. Then they can add to the table a description of the flow of control in terms of memory and real-time interactions in the disc.

This kind of table will be a key diagram in designing the software because, whenever something is being shown to the viewer, the programmer will want to use that time to retrieve the next image or sound from the disc. Tables, diagrams and so on can help the programming team to illustrate the fact that two or more activities may be going on at the same time.

Here is a CD-I producer working out in practical terms how the memory requirement for his title can be managed:

'We assume that the interface data will occupy about 275 kilobytes. Two to three font modules, occupying about 175 kB, will be loaded to allow different fonts to be displayed simultaneously, and the graphics will occupy 107 kB. Program code will occupy less than 150 kB and program data (synchronization tables and so on) will occupy less than 100 kB. Text data for the program, including all the files to support the features outlined above, must therefore occupy less than 150 kB. This leaves a margin of roughly 60 kB to allow some flexibility between titles. In practice, this margin might be used to preload the interface for the programmable CD-DA controller device, which would allow quick response to a request that is likely to be made often.'

OS-9 and CD-RTOS

OS-9 is a real-time multitasking operating system. CD-RTOS is a customized version of OS-9, produced by Microware to run on all CD-I players.

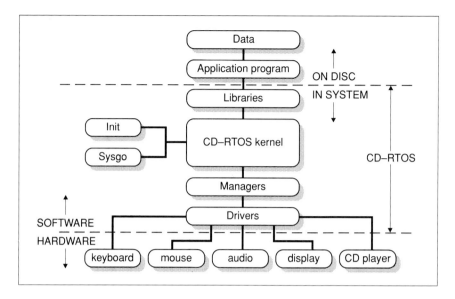

Figure 9.2 CD-RTOS organization.

CD-RTOS contains file managers to support the compact disc drive, multimedia equipment, system memory and all the communications that take place between components and processes. It is a modular operating system, so compatible OS-9 system modules and applications can be loaded while OS-9 is in use.

The shell interface

CD-RTOS provides a UNIX-type shell command interpreter. This provides users with a high-level interface to the internal functions of the CD-RTOS operating system (Figure 9.2). The shell utilities set contains over 70 commands that allow the programmer to set the user environment, memory allocation, input/output redirection, process monitoring, wildcard pattern search, multitasking, file manipulation, timekeeping and text-editing.

OS-9 commands can be batched together into procedure files that can run as background tasks. The input/output system is interrupt-driven: instead of polling the input devices to see whether an event has happened, it is in a continual state of readiness to deal with an event. This is necessary if it is to handle real-time events effectively.

Tools

CD-RTOS has a library of device drivers, so that it can support many types of input/output devices. CD-RTOS also supports C and gives access to powerful assembler, linker and debugger facilities. It has a range of extra tools, such as special display-screen managers, a presentation support library, multimedia file managers, C source and assembly-level tools. It also has a simple-to-use cross-C and assembly tool for transferring programs written under MS-DOS to the CD-RTOS environment.

Conclusion

Programming is a technically demanding phase of CD-I development that requires specialist input, either from dedicated programmers or staff who are sufficiently experienced with CD-I authoring systems to get the best out of them. There are a growing number of robust, mature programming tools to enable programmers to solve many of the problems they may encounter, and to ease and automate the development task.

As well as completing the current disc project, programmers should look to future projects and try to build a library of reusable software routines and engines for use in them. This not only saves time and money in the long term but enables a studio to build up a recognizable style for its programmes.

10
Disc-building to disc-pressing

Introduction

This chapter looks at building a disc image and the production processes that follow, the equipment that is available to make testing disc images simpler and the importance of testing and validation in successful CD-I development and production.

A disc image may consist of several real-time files and non-real-time files such as soundmaps, computer data and so on. We look first at the real-time files and how they are produced from the audio, video and other data gathered for the programme and stored on the computer (Figure 10.1).

Disc-building

Programmers using a full set of authoring tools, such as those provided by CD-I Author, have an active involvement in building the disc.

CD-I Author has a disc-building utility, called Master/Ready. It reads all the files that the programmer has listed in a specially written script and produces a single large file called the disc image. This is formatted as a single data stream that corresponds to the spiral of data that will eventually be etched onto

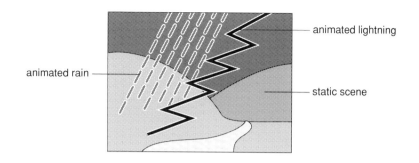

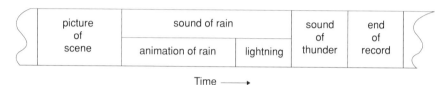

Time ──────▶

Figure 10.1 Part of a real-time file.

the master optical disc. Master/Ready organizes pictures, data and sound so that they are played back in synchronization, and interactivity operates correctly.

Clearly, getting this data stream right will take up a large part of the programmer's time. Disc-building, along with emulation (described on page 134 below), is a key process in CD-I production.

Interleaving

The organization of the data stream, interleaving, was discussed earlier on (page 45). As well as interleaving, the disc-building utility adds technical information that will be needed for emulation or mastering. It notes which sectors in the real-time file should be accessed for file retrieval and which sectors contain information on the disc label, directories and paths. It also breaks the file down into tracks, each separated by pauses or gaps. The disc-builder also usually produces a **map report**,

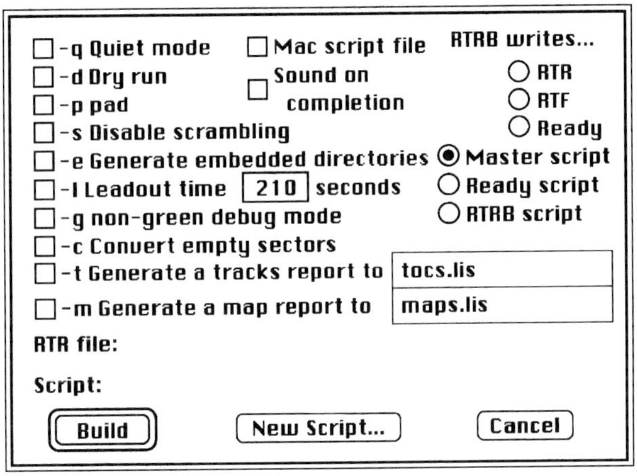

Figure 10.2 A screen displayed by the Master/Ready
utility of CD-I Author.

describing the sector allocation in the real-time file that forms
the disc image (Figure 10.2).

'Although programmers need to be aware of the interleaving
process, it's handled automatically by the software. For programmers the problem is writing the runtime software to handle
the way the data has been laid down on the disc,' says a CD-I
programmer.

Structure of a real-time file

In this section, we look in more detail at how the real-time file
is structured.

A real-time file is made up of real-time records that in turn are
composed of real-time sectors. The real-time sectors are the basic
building-blocks of the file. Correctly digitally converted files and
code, produced from script-to-disc software or an authoring
system, will be in the format specified in the Green Book.

Sectors may also contain a **signal bit**. For example, a real-time record consists of a sequence of sectors that finishes with a sector containing an end-of-record signal bit. This is carried in the sector header and causes a software interrupt of the program that is running (see Figure 4.5). Other examples of signal bits are end-of-file bits and trigger bits, which initiate loading of new video, audio and so on. The signal bits in the real-time sectors are a vital mechanism in synchronizing audio, video and program information.

Realistically, because motion video takes up more space than audio, a real-time file might contain a repeated sequence of 12 sectors of video, interleaved with one or two of audio, then a space for loading the application code. For instance, context-sensitive help might be loaded into the player between blocks of audio and video.

However, it is in fact the requirements of the audio that drive the interleaving process. Audio data within a real-time record, whether it is being loaded from disc or from RAM, must arrive at the audio processor at exact intervals. If it does not, it will not be heard by the listener as realistic sound. The audio sectors in the real-time record are rather like a clock with which the other elements, such as video, are synchronized. So the audio sectors are allocated first: the empty sectors between these can be used for video or text, which need less precise timing. Obviously, you could also alternate different audio tracks – for instance, commentary in French and commentary in English.

When a real-time record is read, the sectors are sorted and directed by the compact-disc file manager. For instance, all the audio sectors are sent for output through the audio channels. Sectors containing computer data are always read into memory, to be processed by an application program.

Creating a real-time file

A software utility is used to construct the real-time files from the basic audio and video files held on the hard disk. The utility makes sure that the sectors are spaced so that the material will play correctly. It also adds the sector headers and other information described in the previous section.

The disc-building tool will 'play' this script by building a real-time file, in which the audio and video materials are interleaved into a single stream of data sectors, arriving at the player in the correctly ordered sequence.

Some prototyping tools allow you quite a lot of say in precisely how the interleaving is organized. There is a familiar tradeoff here, between simplicity and control. Tools that produce a real-time file automatically are simpler to use but those that let you build it by hand give you more control. If you want to fine-tune the layout of the disc, you will need to use an environment that allows direct access to the disc layout.

For instance, MacTrack, which runs in the Apple Macintosh environment, builds the CD-I real-time file to custom specifications. A dialogue box gives a graphic representation of the sectors in part of the disc. The user can click on the sectors and rearrange them, until satisfied with them.

As with many CD-I tradeoffs, there are costs and benefits to each alternative. Sophisticated disc layout and interleaving can liberate storage space, but this has its costs: the more sophisticated the layout, the harder it is to write the controlling software. Many experienced CD-I programmers believe that the simplest approach is often the best, and should be chosen unless disc space is at a premium.

Many script-to-disc conversion tools do not give this level of access to the interleaving process. Instead they carry out interleaving automatically. This is an extremely efficient and painless way to produce a CD-I title. Of course, you cannot fine-tune the interleaved file in the way you can if you are programming. However, you can adjust the individual start and end timings of the audio and video files, or separate the files into smaller modules.

For some applications, automatic interleaving is all that's needed. Beware unnecessary complexity. A custom-built interleaved real-time file may have its attractions but it will add considerably to the programmers' workload, which may cause additional problems in meeting deadlines at this stage of the production process.

Building the disc image

As well as working out the best sequencing for the audio and video sectors, the authoring system automatically builds the disc. In other words, it works out where on the optical disc the interleaved sequences should be stored so that the video and audio data reaches the player's processors at the correct moment. In doing so, the authoring system takes account of factors such as disc access.

During this 'lay-out' process, the interleaved sequences are positioned in a linear track, so that they can be output as an exact image of the spiral of data that will eventually form the finished compact disc. This process is the most demanding part of CD-I production as far as the computer hardware is concerned.

A massive amount of storage space is required for all the data being moved around. One CD-I programmer says:

'Building real-time files from the programme assets can get through four to five times the amount of space used by the final disc image. If you don't have enough storage it can cause logistical problems, to say nothing of denting the budget if you need to buy an extra hard disk.'

Script-to-disc software converts the logical script produced by an authoring system such as MediaMogul to a file format that can be included in the disc image when it is built. The disc-building utility reads the IFF file header of each file and processes it appropriately, according to its contents.

Amending the disc image

Once the disc image has been created on the computer's hard disk, it can be tested. In fact, authors will carry out this disc-building process dozens of times as they follow the script/play/amend script/play process by which they achieve the effects they are aiming at. If, for instance, a piece of audio plays too soon, it can be fixed and a new disc image built. This is done by resetting the trigger bit so that the audio is started at a different absolute time.

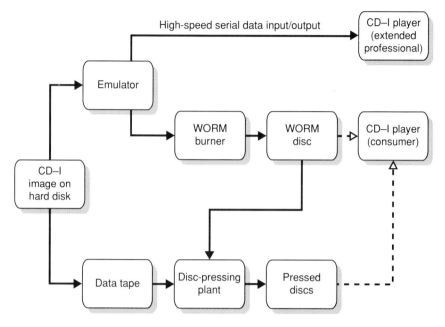

Figure 10.3 Using a disc image.

After amending the disc image, you remaster and produce a new disc image. There are then three things you can do with it (Figure 10.3):

- use it for emulation
- use it to make a WORM disc
- send it off for production of the CD-I

We now look at these processes in more detail.

Emulation

Authors tend to spend most of their time testing and amending their applications. Obviously, it is not worth creating an optical disc in order to do this when the data is actually stored on the workstation or PC. Disc emulation solves this problem. In disc emulation, the disc image is passed to an emulator. This passes the data to the CD-I player, in exactly the same format as the real-time data stream produced by an optical disc, so that you can play the title even though all the audio-visual materials and code are still on the hard disk of a PC.

Once the emulation process has started and the appropriate data is being fed to the player, the application is fully 'active'. All the interactive routines will work with the player's user interface.

In this section, we will look at the example of a workstation or PC, with a hard disk, connected via an emulator to a CD-I player. The CD-I disc image is built on the PC and accessed directly from its SCSI disk by the emulator hardware. The PC stops and starts the emulator, via commands sent down a connecting serial cable. During emulation, the emulator sends status reports that are displayed on the PC's screen.

The workstation-based emulation software actually consists of two programs. The first, called **discmap**, outputs a sector map of the disc image file. The second, **emulate**, is a shell program. It calls **discmap**, then starts the emulator.

The emulator is simply connected to the programmer's workstation by the SCSI bus, which might also link other devices, such as hard disks, tapes or a WORM drive.

How emulation works

When the programmer or author 'plays' the title, the multimedia controller in the CD-I player (see box) asks for information about where the data sectors are located. The request is passed on via the emulator box, and the data is retrieved from the disc image file in the programmer's workstation. Acknowledgments are exchanged between the hard disk and the emulator. Further requests for data are passed from the player to the PC via the emulator and the data is passed from the PC to the emulator, which passes it to the player's multimedia controller at the rate of 172 kilobytes per second.

> ### The multimedia controller
> The multimedia controller is part of the CD-I player and provides
> its control system. It consists of a megabyte of dynamic RAM and
> a 68000-family microprocessor. It has video and audio outputs
> and communicates with the CD in the player's drive, sending
> instructions and receiving data. It often has a bus expansion plug.
> The multimedia controller communicates with the emulator via a
> special serial line.

The emulator has an optional built-in SCSI hard disk, which can
be used for storing data so that you need not have a second hard
disk on your host computer.

The emulator is actually another computer with its own 68020
processor. It communicates with a workstation PC or Macintosh
via an SCSI interface and with the player via a serial cable. Like
dedicated CD-I players it uses OS-9 and CD-RTOS operating
systems, although it is attached to host workstations that use their
own operating systems. The use of an emulator is therefore one
of the main ways of building a bridge between the two operating
systems to allow them to communicate with each other.

Hardware emulators can be attached to all the types of
computer likely to be used in CD-I development: the Apple
Macintosh II series, IBM 386 and 486 PCs and compatibles, the
Sun 4 series (including the SunSparc Station 1), and other UNIX
systems.

Using the disc image to produce a WORM

The emulator provides a signal that looks to the player exactly
like the signal from an optical disc. However, it cannot provide
accurate information on access times – how long the disc takes
to track between various items on the disc. This information can
only be accurately assessed if the disc image is used to produce
a WORM and the WORM is tested.

Worm drives

A WORM disc can be cut by a standard drive. The specially coated discs are spun under a high-powered laser beam and the laser 'burns' a pattern of pits onto the surface of the disc. WORM discs are useful in circumstances where you do not need to go in for full-scale CD production, such as:

- when prototyping
- when only a few discs are needed (as in some training, point-of-sale or point-of-information applications)
- when the discs are being used to archive data
- as an interim stage, for user testing

Using the disc image as a master

The disc image is checked and verified (a process described in more detail in the next section). When both the development team and the client are satisfied, the data stream is recorded on an 8-mm Exabyte tape, nine-track tape or WORM disc. These are used as the masters for replication at a disc-pressing plant.

Testing and validation

The final disc image may be transferred to a few optical WORM discs, which can be tested with the intended audience. Most producers issue the users with a standard validation reporting form on which they can record problems and queries.

Much current CD-I testing is also carried out by members of the production team, who sit down with the title specification and work through it on a module-by-module basis, with some global testing towards the end. The more time and money the production team is prepared to spend on testing, the more thorough it can be – but it can never be complete.

However, in a bid to speed up and rationalize the testing process, some producers have developed automated testing. They videotape people using the title, then gather information on the parts of the title that were most successful, those that caused problems, and so on.

Another method of testing currently being tried out is to record user activity by means of a mouse or other interface device. The movements of the device can be tracked, recorded and analysed to provide information on how the screens are being used.

At the production plant

At the plant, the data is read from the master medium, whether it is a tape or a WORM disc. This information is then etched onto the surface of the blank master CD-I discs, in a series of pits that will eventually be read by the player's laser.

Disc replication and the production of packaging need to be scheduled so that the two processes are coordinated. It is very important that clear agreement is reached in advance as to:

● who is responsible for the label art

● who is responsible for the packaging and any supplementary materials

Typically, a disc-pressing plant will provide a standard CD-I that looks like the one in Figure 10.4. The labelling comprises:

● customer information – this will be limited to, for instance, three lines with 22 characters per line

● disc title – the maximum length of this will probably be around 30 characters

● CD-I and disc-presser's logo

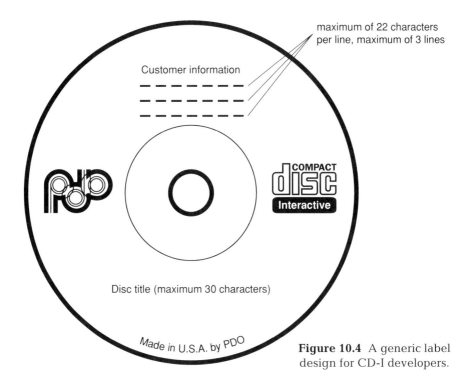

Figure 10.4 A generic label design for CD-I developers.

Title artwork and the use of colour will need to be thought out very carefully. It is common for the standard information on the disc to be provided in black and the customer-specific information to be printed in one colour from a standard colour chart.

For many applications, such as training, this is sufficient. But if you want to make your CD-I as eye-catching as possible, you will probably want the entire CD-I label to be custom-artworked. Most pressing plants will accept positive films. However, you should get in touch with the plant at an early stage, to discuss your design and make sure that it is suitable for CD-I use.

Many pressing plants provide a mastering package that includes services such as two-colour printing of custom artwork. More colours can be used but will, of course, be more expensive. Some pressing plants now also offer half-tone graphics and colour photography. If high-quality artwork is important for your title it is well worth researching this area before you book the job.

Bear in mind also that using custom art labelling will add to the turn-round time for the disc-pressing. The plant will probably want you to deliver camera-ready artwork, or film, well before the master arrives at the plant.

The pressing plant will supply 'jewel cases', the clear plastic cases in which the CD-I will be sold. Any printed material to be inserted into the jewel case must be ready well in advance.

Conclusion

The final stages of the CD-I production process are technically the most demanding of the equipment and, indeed, the staff. Most producers will let their software sort out the complex business of turning script and contents into the final format that will be pressed onto the CD-I disc. Others may find that their programme requires a human touch to get it working in exactly the right way.

At this stage the final round of testing should begin and should not be skimped on. As with any large-scale project, last-minute frustrations do occur; elements of the programme can interact in an unexpected manner, so that the result is not as pleasing as expected. Thorough testing with prototypes and working to a clear specification may have reduced the likelihood of problems at the end of the production process, but it's still a good idea to test the disc image before it goes to the pressing plant.

11

The next project

Introduction

Most of this book has been concerned with the development and production of a first CD-I programme. In reality, CD-I producers will be working on several projects, either concurrently or consecutively. While the advice contained in the previous chapters still applies, producers can develop ways of working to improve the efficiency and the ease with which programmes can be made.

The benefits of experience should allow CD-I producers to streamline some phases of the production process; programming is probably the aspect most responsive to this approach. However, all parts of design and development can be carried out with an eye to the production of series of programmes, sequels and associated titles. Guidelines covering different aspects of production can lay down house style and methodology and provide a quick way of answering many questions that pop up during the course of design and production.

Sequels

One of the best pieces of advice for CD-I designers is to design with sequels in mind. A sequel is a cost-efficient way of capitalizing on the success of a previous title. However, if the first programme was produced with no thought of possible sequels this becomes more difficult, because more of the production and design effort will have to be duplicated.

Planning a series of discs right from the start of design and development means that more resources can be spent on developing the programmes. Software engines, and even programme structure and interface design, can be shared across the titles, so that economies of scale can be achieved, and more effort can be expended than would be possible for a single title.

Some programmes will always be one-offs, which can't result in second and subsequent programmes. However, the format of these programmes could be reused with very different material. It may only be possible to make one programme about the career of a particular musician, but the same format could be applied to other performers.

House style

Some CD-I studios have evolved firm guidelines covering every aspect of CD-I production. This helps to ensure the quality and recognizability of the finished product; there are advantages to working in a clearly identifiable style.

Guidelines could cover anything from the way the budget is split between different areas of production to detailed rules for user interface design. One CD-I production studio uses its style guide for three purposes:

- to promote good interactive design
- to exploit the strengths and avoid the weaknesses of CD-I
- to ensure consistency across the growing range of titles it has produced

Its style book contains advice on everything from menu layout to ways of avoiding sexist language; without stifling creativity or innovation, it provides a clear framework within which creative and production staff can work.

It's important that guidelines don't become a straitjacket and prevent designers and production staff from making innovative contributions to projects. The studio may always have done things a certain way in the past, but a different approach might benefit a particular project.

If the style guide evolves from the working practices and the experience of the team it is more likely to be used. There are many questions that can easily be answered by reference to a well thought-out style guide. Traditional style guides cover editorial matters such as preferred spellings and punctuation formats; a CD-I style guide can include these as well as providing guidance on consistency of menu screens and other items specific to CD-I.

Software efficiency

Programming is an area where real economies can be made with a little foresight, if producers are prepared to devote sufficient resources to allow the programming team to analyse current and future requirements and spend time developing code that can be reused.

Developing reusable code provides benefits beyond the economic ones. Using mature and proven code reduces the likelihood of errors and could further cut the development time. More effort can then be expended on other aspects of the programme, such as games and other unique segments that will need a lot of programming effort.

Consistency between programmes is improved if they are based on the same software engines, and this makes them easier to use and to support.

Conclusion

Producers can implement a variety of strategies to create an organized CD-I production environment, with well-defined working practices designed to cope with any foreseeable problems and difficulties. As a studio becomes established and starts to produce many CD-I programmes, the same problems are likely to crop up more than once, and the existence of studio guidelines can provide a quick resolution.

Guidelines are also immensely useful for ensuring consistency in style and quality across the programmes produced by a studio. They may provide creative as well as practical advice and prevent designers and producers from having to reinvent the wheel with every new project.

Good programming practice has always revolved around writing code that can be reused. It is easier to manage, becomes more and more reliable, and saves a great deal of effort and resources in the medium and long term, even if it seems strange that programmers are working on a code segment that is not directly applicable to the current project.

However, as the studio settles into successful CD-I production and becomes more and more familiar with the tools and technical possibilities associated with the medium, it is important to remain open to new ideas. CD-I continues to develop, and producers should be alert not only to (for example) the availability of new and improved authoring tools but to the growing number of finished programmes and the range of styles they represent. Interactive television is just beginning; there is great scope for innovative studios both to maintain current production standards and to improve on the exciting discs now appearing.

Further reading

Collier D. (1991). *Collier's Rules for Desktop Design and Typography*. Wokingham: Addison-Wesley

Laurel B., ed. (1990). *The Art of Human-Computer Interface Design*. Reading, MA: Addison-Wesley

Laurel B. (1991). *Computers as Theatre*. Reading, MA: Addison-Wesley

Philips International (1987). *Compact Disc Interactive: A Designer's Overview*. Deventer: Kluwer Technical Books

Rubin T. (1988). *User Interface Design for Computer Systems*. Chichester: Ellis Horwood

Woodhead N. (1990). *Hypertext and Hypermedia: Theory and Applications*. Wilmslow: Sigma Press, Wokingham: Addison-Wesley

Glossary

Terms appearing in *italic* type within an entry have their own definitions in the Glossary.

Adaptive delta pulse code modulator All audio signals used by CD-I use a method of digital encoding known as Adaptive Delta Pulse Code Modulation (ADPCM). This involves sampling the sound and encoding the difference between successive samples. Before it can be played back the data has to be decoded.

ADPCM See *Adaptive delta pulse code modulator*

Analogue/digital Analogue and digital are two methods of recording and displaying data. When Caruso sang into the horn of a gramophone, making a vibrating needle cut directly into a wax cylinder, that was analogue recording. When Pavarotti sings into a microphone and his voice is recorded as a series of numerical values, that is digital recording. The difference is that analogue methods of recording or displaying information are continuously variable, while digital methods break the information up into small bits (pulses). A watch with hands is an analogue display, while a watch with numbers is digital. Analogue methods of recording and reproduction tend to cause degradation (for example, photocopying), while digital methods are proof against this.

Application The use of a technology (such as CD-I) for a specific purpose, often in the form of a commercial software package. For example, a 'how-to-drive' CD-I is a training application, and MediaMogul is a multimedia production application.

Aspect ratio The way in which shapes appearing on a screen are distorted by the proportions of the pixels making up the screen. Some pixels are square (for example, on Apple Macintosh machines), and some are rectangular. This means that the data that appears as a circle on one screen will appear oval on another. The mathematical expression of the distortion occurring in this way is called the aspect ratio and should be taken into consideration when designing for the screen.

Audio quality level There are four sound quality formats in CD-I. The highest is CD-DA, the quality of an ordinary CD. It uses all the available bandwidth. Level A is equivalent to the sort of sound quality you obtain when you play a brand-new LP on good-quality equipment, although without any of the background hiss. You can get two hours of stereo or four hours of mono level A sound on a CD-I disc. Level B sound is equivalent to a first-class FM radio broadcast. You can get up to four hours of stereo level B sound on a CD-I disc. Level C is more like AM radio received under good conditions. It is completely adequate for speech. You can get about nine hours of level C stereo audio on a CD-I disc.

Authoring Producing a CD-I programme, from concept to master tape. Authoring can also be used to apply more specifically to the electronic stages of the process, such as editing.

Authoring platform A combination of a machine and some software that is used to stitch together and create the links in CD-I programmes. It also allows *emulation* of the programme and may include some graphics facilities for creating *menus*, text pages and so on.

Bandwidth Bandwidth is the speed at which data can be transferred from the CD-I disc and used by the player. The CD-I player can read 75 data *sectors* per second, which is 172 kilobytes of data per second. The speed at which data is read becomes crucial when a lot of data has to be transferred – for example, when high-quality images and sound are used at the same time, or if there are several sound tracks running parallel to allow switching between them in *real time*.

Blind A two-plane visual effect in which the image on the front plane becomes like a Venetian blind that opens to reveal the image on the back plane. See *Picture planes*.

Branching Moving away from one part of a CD-I programme to another. This is usually in response to user interaction.

Byte A piece of data that is 7 or 8 bits long. 1024 bytes make one kilobyte (abbreviated as K or KB), and 1024 kilobytes make a megabyte (abbreviated as MB).

CD-DA Compact Disc Digital Audio. Uses the compact disc format for storing high-quality digital audio.

CD-I Compact Disc Interactive.

CD-ROM Compact Disc Read-Only Memory. Uses the large storage capacity of a CD disc to store digitally encoded data. This is usually text, and is used in electronic publishing for databases and reference works.

CD-ROM XA Compact Disc Read-Only Memory Extended Architecture. Uses the large storage capacity of a CD disc to store digitally encoded data. The extended architecture is used to interleave blocks of text, images, music and program data.

CD-RTOS Compact Disc Real-Time Operating System, the CD-I operating system. CD-RTOS is a flexible modularized system that can run a large number of programs at the same time, and so is particularly suited to CD-I applications.

Channel A channel is the path along which information flows from the CD-I disc to the player. CD-I can handle up to 16 audio channels and

32 channels for other purposes (for example, video, software and so on). The size of a channel is called its *bandwidth*.

Chroma key A two-*picture plane* technique that makes a selected colour or colours on the front plane transparent so that the image on the back plane can be seen through it. So, for example, a person can be filmed against a background of a certain colour, and chroma key can be used to make this background invisible so that a different background can be used.

CLUT See *Colour Look-Up Table*.

Colour Look-Up Table (CLUT) A matrix containing the colours that can be used in an image. Because each colour in the table can be referred to by its position in the table instead of by specifying its absolute colour value, this is an effective way of saving storage space on the disc. There are three types of CLUT: CLUT 8, CLUT 7 and CLUT 4. The table for a CLUT 7 image gives a choice of 128 colours, and that for a CLUT 8 gives 256 colours. This choice can be expanded by using *dynamic updating* – a useful technique in animation. Each single-screen CLUT image takes up the following space in the CD-I player's memory:

PAL or compatibility	105 kilobytes
NTSC	85 kilobytes

Further compression of CLUT images can be achieved by using *RLE*.

Compatibility mode This is the screen specification for a CD-I programme that has to run on both *PAL* and *NTSC* screens. The screen area is 384 × 280 pixels, and the *safe area* is 320 × 210 pixels.

Compression A technique for reducing the amount of data needed on the disc to store images or sounds, or sequences of them. For example, if an image has large areas that are the same colour, instead of the colour of every cell of the picture being recorded, the colour is recorded once, along with its location and the number of cells over which it extends. When the disc is played the image is decompressed before it appears on the screen. There are several different methods of compressing images, which suit different types of image, such as natural images and animated (cartoon) images. These include *DYUV*, *CLUT* and *RLE*.

Curtain A two-plane visual effect in which the image on the front plane parts or closes like a pair of curtains to reveal the image on the back plane. See *Picture planes*.

Cut A one- or two-plane visual effect in which one image disappears and is immediately replaced by a different one, either on the same plane or another. See *Picture planes*.

DAT Digital Audio Tape. A digital audio tape contains up to two hours of continuous digital sound.

DCC Digital Compact Cassette tape. Digitally recorded tape that has the same high quality as DAT, but has the advantage of using the existing standard tape cassette.

Delta Luminance Colour Difference See *DYUV*.

Digital See *Analogue/digital.*

Dynamic updating A technique used with CLUT images to increase the number of colours available. As each line of the screen is painted, the Colour Look-Up Table is changed. Thus instead of the 256 colours normally available from a single CLUT 8 image, a range of over 1000 colours can be obtained in a single image.

DYUV Delta Luminance Colour Difference, a compression technique for storing image data. Instead of recording the absolute colour value of each cell or pixel of the image, it stores only the relative differences in brightness (known as Y) and colour (known as U and V) between adjacent cells. You can have DYUV images on both *picture planes* at the same time to achieve plane effects. Each single whole-screen image takes up the following space in the CD-I player's memory:

PAL or compatibility mode	105 kilobytes
NTSC	85 kilobytes

DYUV images are suitable for storing 'natural' images, such as photographs.

Emulation The playback process used during development of CD-I titles. The title is developed on the hard disk of the computer. To play it back as if it were a real CD-I disc being played on a CD-I player, a program called an emulator is used, which enables the computer to imitate a CD-I player. This is one of the best ways of judging whether the programme is working in the way you intended.

Fade up/down A one-plane visual effect in which the image fades into blankness before being replaced by the next image. See also *Picture planes.*

Flowchart A technique used by computer software designers and others to represent sequences of events in a program, using drawings of boxes representing program elements, connected by directional lines.

Font A set of letter shapes used for displaying text – for example, Times Roman. There are two ways of displaying text in CD-I: either using the resident font of the system, which is satisfactory for utilitarian functions such as displaying system messages; or by downloading a chosen font at runtime, and using that to display text. The second technique is obviously more suitable for text displays where the appearance of the letters is important.

Full motion A video image that moves naturally and without jerkiness. Smooth motion normally requires a frame speed of at least 25 frames per second. A CD-I disc will hold approximately 72 minutes of full-motion video. This can be increased if only a part of the screen is used to display the moving image (*partial-screen video*). See also *Partial motion.*

Green Book Two volumes in which all the specifications of the standard for CD-I players and discs are contained. The standard is subscribed to by Philips, Sony and other key manufacturers, and is to CD-I what the Red Book standard was to CD-DA discs.

Hotspot An area of the screen that is used to make selections and choices in a CD-I programme. Typically, the user uses the remote control to move the pointer on the screen to the hotspot, and clicks a button to make a choice. The hotspot is often a menu button, though it can be some other object, such as an icon.

HyperCard An information tool developed by Apple for its Macintosh range of personal computers, which allows you to store different types of data (still and moving video, graphics, text, music, animation, speech) on 'cards' . The cards are held in stacks and can be accessed in a number of different ways, according to different topics and methods of classification. HyperCard can be a useful *prototyping* tool for testing the logic of a CD-I program.

Hypermedia A way of storing information so that it can be referenced and used in a nonlinear manner, one point of information being accessed directly from another without the need to go to an intervening index or table of contents. Apple's HyperCard program is probably the best-known commercial hypermedia tool.

Icon An icon is a small picture or image that stands for something. For example, an hourglass on the screen might mean that a process is going on and you have to wait. Icons are a useful nonverbal way of showing what is happening or what you need to do. You can use icons with hotspots to enliven the process of making interactive choices for the audience.

Interactive multimedia The combination of *interactivity* with *multimedia* enables the audience or user to make choices and control the pace, direction and content of a programme. CD-I is interactive multimedia.

Interactivity The flow of input and output between two systems: in the case of CD-I, between the user and the CD-I player and disc. The user's choices control the pace, direction, content and other aspects of a multimedia programme.

Interface The interface is the place where a system meets its user. This happens on two levels: first at the hardware level, where the interface is the type of equipment used (for example: remote control, keyboard, touch–screen); second at the software level, where it is the way the system appears to the user (for example: menus, hotspots and so on). A well-designed interface is essential to make a programme usable and attractive to viewers.

Interleaving A way in which the *sectors* on a CD-I disc can be arranged that allows all the information necessary for the pictures and sounds in the programme to be read at the right time. So, for example, if a programme demands parallel sound tracks in different languages, sectors making up the image and the different sound tracks will be *interleaved*, or woven together on the disc.

Kilobyte (Kb) A kilobyte is 1024 *bytes.* 1024 kilobytes make one *megabyte.*

Lipsynch The *synchronization* of lip movements on screen with speech sounds on the soundtrack.

Mastering The production of the master disc, from which copies can be made. See *Replication.*

Matte A two-plane visual effect in which a defined area of the front plane is made transparent, revealing the image on the back plane. See *Picture planes.*

Megabyte (Mb) Approximately a million *bytes* of data. The resident memory of the CD-I player has a capacity of one megabyte, divided into 512 kilobytes for each of the two *Picture planes.*

Menu A menu is a list of items on screen from which the user can choose. In an interactive system this can be one way of enabling the user to interact. Each item is accompanied by a button; the user moves the pointer to the button and clicks the remote control to make a choice.

Mosaic Mosaics are single-*picture plane* effects that are used in images to achieve two types of result: progressive coarsening of the image until it is dissolved (pixel hold); and enlargement of the image (pixel repeat).

Multimedia A medium employing the combination and recombination of elements in a number of individual media, such as video, audio, text and graphics. The process relies upon a computer to bring these elements together and make them into a coherent product. See also *Interactive multimedia.*

National Television Standards Committee See *NTSC.*

Natural image Pictures that are photographic and appear realistic.

Non-Volatile Random Access Memory See *NVRAM.*

NTSC The standard for television pictures in the United States. (The acronym stands for National Television Standards Committee.) The picture size for images to play on NTSC television sets is 360 × 240 pixels, and the *safe area* is 320 × 210 pixels. See also *PAL* and *Compatibility mode.*

NVRAM Non-Volatile Random Access Memory. NVRAM is a small permanent memory in the CD-I player that can be used to store data that you do not want to lose when the machine is switched off. This could be, for example, password information or game scores. The CD-I player's NVRAM holds eight kilobytes of data. See also *Personal memory card.*

PAL Phase Alternating Line. The standard for television pictures in the UK, most of Europe, Australia and South America. The picture size for images to play on PAL television sets is 384 × 280 pixels, and the *safe area* is 320 × 250 pixels. See also *NTSC* and *Compatibility mode.*

Partial motion The use of a series of still images at a speed of less than approximately 20 frames per second to achieve a jerky sort of motion. This makes fewer demands upon the capacities of the CD-I player and disc, and is actually more suitable than *full motion* for some applications, such as slowed-down procedures (mending a tap) or surrogate walks.

Partial-screen video The use of only part of the screen for some purpose. This is a good way of saving disc space when you are using full-motion video. For example, if you have a window of full-motion video that takes up 40% of the screen area, you will need only 40% as much memory to store the moving video image.

Partial updating The CD-I player screen can be divided horizontally into a number of *subscreens*. Each of these can hold pictures of a different type (for example, CLUT and DYUV images can be in subscreens of the same screen), and can be updated or changed separately from the other subscreens.

Personal memory card An optional extra permanent memory for some CD-I players, which slots into the front. It can be used when an application or programme needs to store more information than the system's resident permanent memory (*NVRAM*) can hold.

Phase alternating line See *PAL*.

Picture planes Manipulation of moving and still images on the CD-I screen is enhanced by the use of the picture planes, arranged one behind another. Altogether there are four picture planes: at the very front is the cursor plane, which holds a cursor of up to 16 × 16 pixels; behind that are the two image planes, each able to hold an image of up to 512 kilobytes; and at the back is a plane that can be a single colour, or can be used to hold a video image from a source outside the CD-I player. The two middle planes, the image planes, are the most important. A number of effects such as *curtains*, *blinds* and *mattes,* can be used to change between the images on the two planes, or to show parts of images from both planes.

Pixel A contraction of 'picture element'. The basic cell or unit of a television or computer-screen picture. The number and size of pixels available on a screen dictate the resolution of the image. To make an image the colour and brightness of each cell must be specified. Pixels can be manipulated as the basis for *mosaic* picture effects. See also *NTSC, PAL*.

Pointer The small object on the screen that can be moved around – for example, by using the *remote control*. Typically, the pointer is used to point to an item on a menu, which is then selected by clicking a button on the pointing device.

Program A computer program controls and organizes the contents of the CD-I *programme.*

Programme For the purposes of this book a CD-I production, like its relatives on radio or television, is called a programme.

Prototyping As with any product, a sort of working model may the best way of checking whether it is going to work or not. When designing a CD-I disc, certain authoring platforms may be used to construct a simple prototype before production commences in earnest.

Real time Real-time areas of the CD-I programme are ones that are played as they are read. For example, audio material is read from the disc, processed and played in real time. Images first pass into the player's memory, where they are accessed as required by the control program, and are not real-time. *Interleaving* techniques for arranging data on the CD-I disc make it possible for users to switch between audio *channels* in real time. For example, if a guide-disc has parallel language tracks, it is possible to design the disc so that the user can switch between languages instantaneously.

Remote control The physical device that the CD-I viewer uses to control and interact with a programme. Typically, it looks like the remote control for a video player or a television, with the addition of a small joystick. The joystick is used to move the *pointer* around the screen.

Replication The manufacturing process by which copies of the master CD-I disc are made.

RGB Red Green Blue. The complete name for this image coding technique is RGB 5:5:5. For each *pixel* the amounts of red, green and blue are specified using five bits of data, giving 32 levels of intensity for each component, or 32,768 colours in total. This technique is suitable for very high-quality images – such as reproductions of paintings – but uses the whole of the CD-I player's memory, so that you can only use one *picture plane* with RGB images.

RLE A technique, run-length encoding, of compressing the amount of memory space needed to store the data for recording an image. This technique records only the value of the colour and the number of pixels over which it extends in each line. So a line of the screen in which there is only one colour would need only two bytes of data storage instead of one byte per pixel, as in CLUT 7 and CLUT 8 images. The degree of compression achieved by RLE depends upon the complexity of the image being stored in this way.

Rolling demo A segment of a CD-I programme that can be used at retail outlets or exhibitions to show what the programme is and what it does, and to sample its look and feel.

Run-length encoding See *RLE*.

Safe area The safe area of the CD-I screen is the area in which you can place hotspots or menu buttons where they will not be affected by the edge of the screen. The size of the safe area varies according to the television standard in use (*PAL* or *NTSC*). For CD-I programmes to play on both types of receiver, use the *compatibility mode* safe area. The safe areas are as follows:

PAL	320×250 pixels
NTSC and compatibility mode	320×210 pixels

Scrolling A useful way of presenting large images on the CD-I screen and giving the illusion of a camera panning across them. In fact what happens is that the whole image is loaded into the player's memory, and is presented piece by piece on the screen. Thus by scrolling an image of the Leaning Tower of Pisa downwards, you would present the illusion of a camera panning upwards.

SECAM The standard for television pictures used in France. The acronym stands for *Système Electronique Couleur Avec Mémoire*. As far as CD-I production is concerned it is equivalent to PAL.

Sector An area of the CD-I disc containing data. Each sector contains approximately two kilobytes of data, and the player can read 75 sectors per second. A sector can contain audio, video or text, as well as control data. Different types of sector are interleaved to assist real-time playback (see *Interleaving*). Sectors on the disc are arranged in *tracks*. The disc should be laid out so that tracks containing closely associated material are near each other, thus minimizing *seek time*.

Seek time The time taken by the CD-I player's laser pickup to move from one track or sector on the disc to another. If the disc is well laid out – that is, if tracks and sectors holding material that is closely related are arranged so that they are close to each other – seek times should be small. The maximum seek time is approximately three seconds.

Software engine A piece of software that carries out a particular task within a CD-I programme – for example, producing a dissolve between the images on the front and back picture planes or, on a higher level, arranging for a sequence of pictures with accompanying audio to be presented. The software engine is standardized and can be used repeatedly wherever required.

Soundmap A small fragment of sound that is stored in the CD-I player's memory. This can be used to reduce the amount of data the player has to read off the CD-I disc and process. The soundmap can be anything from bird-song or applause to a few bars of a tune that can be looped to make longer sound effects. Soundmaps are also useful for gongs and whistles that confirm and reinforce audience choices.

Sprite A small shape that can be moved around the screen under programme control. This can be anything from a fancy cursor or pointer to a font used for displaying text.

Square A two-plane visual effect in which the image on the front plane becomes a square opening or closing, revealing the image on the back plane. See *Picture planes*.

Storyboard The picture-by-picture 'script' for the visual aspects of a CD-I programme. Storyboarding is a technique familiar from the world of film and television.

Subscreen A horizontal division of the CD-I screen in which a specific picture type may be used. For example, different subscreens of the same screen may use *CLUT* and *DYUV* images respectively. The updating of subscreens separately and at different times is known as *partial updating*.

Synchronization For any CD-I production, sound and vision must be correctly lined up at the beginning of each sequence. So, for example, in the case of a talking head lip movements must synchronize with speech sounds (*lipsynch*).

Touch-screen A type of *interface* in which the user touches the screen of the CD-I player to make selections and control the programme. It is ideally suited to point-of-sale and point-of-information systems.

Track The *sectors* on a CD-I disc are arranged in tracks. These are a little like the tracks on an LP and are read sequentially. On a well-laid-out disc, tracks containing closely related material should be close to each other to minimize *seek times*.

Treatment The outline of a CD-I programme that is used to describe the product and to interest potential clients, publishers and so on.

Validation The process of testing a CD-I disc to make sure that it is ready to be distributed.

Video quality Video images can be produced at several levels of quality: *RGB* – suitable for images that require high quality, such as paintings or works of art; *DYUV* – suitable for natural images, such as photographs, requiring a large range of colours; *CLUT* 8 – suitable for computer-generated images, with limited colour range, and backdrops; *CLUT* 7 – suitable for animation; *RLE* – suitable for animation, graphics, text and lettering.

Wipe A two-plane visual effect in which the image on the front plane is rolled back along a horizontal line travelling vertically, or a vertical one travelling horizontally, revealing the image on the back plane. See *Picture planes*.

WORM Write-Once, Read-Many, describing a type of disc that can be recorded on only once. This type of disc is not suitable for mass production, but can be used in small editions or as trial discs for testing and validation purposes.

Index